How to Become a Microcap Millionaire

How to Become a Microcap Millionaire

A three-step strategy for stock market success

✓ What   ✓ When   ✓ How

Justin Waite

Harriman House

HARRIMAN HOUSE LTD
3 Viceroy Court
Bedford Road
Petersfield
Hampshire
GU32 3LJ
GREAT BRITAIN
Tel: +44 (0)1730 233870

Email: enquiries@harriman-house.com
Website: harriman.house

First published in 2024.
Copyright © Justin Waite

The right of Justin Waite to be identified as the Author has been asserted in accordance with the Copyright, Design and Patents Act 1988.

Paperback ISBN: 978-1-80409-142-5
eBook ISBN: 978-1-80409-143-2

British Library Cataloguing in Publication Data
A CIP catalogue record for this book can be obtained from the British Library.

All rights reserved; no part of this publication may be reproduced, stored in a retrieval system, or transmitted in any form or by any means, electronic, mechanical, photocopying, recording, or otherwise without the prior written permission of the Publisher. This book may not be lent, resold, hired out or otherwise disposed of by way of trade in any form of binding or cover other than that in which it is published without the prior written consent of the Publisher.

Whilst every effort has been made to ensure that information in this book is accurate, no liability can be accepted for any loss incurred in any way whatsoever by any person relying solely on the information contained herein.

No responsibility for loss occasioned to any person or corporate body acting or refraining to act as a result of reading material in this book can be accepted by the Publisher, by the Author, or by the employers of the Author.

The Publisher does not have any control over or any responsibility for any Author's or third-party websites referred to in or on this book.

Contents

About the Author	viii
Preface: aka The Cheat Sheet	ix
Introduction	1
1. It's All About Me (Well, This Chapter Is)	5
2. It's a Different Animal	15
3. What Prevents Most People from Becoming Exceptional Investors?	18
4. Risk vs Reward – There Are Two Sides to Every Story	31
5. What, When, How and Where	38
Part One: How	**43**
6. How to Buy: Portfolio Management	45
7. Stop That Loss	57
8. It's Your Money, Manage it Professionally	63
9. The Backbone	66
10. Is Investing Gambling?	75
11. How Many and How Much?	81
12. Winners Keep on Winning, Losers Keep on Losing	90

Part Two: What — 101

13. The What to Buy – Fundamental Research — 103
14. Size Does Matter — 122
15. Always Check the Cash — 126
16. Scoring the Metrics — 131
17. Growth — 133
18. Value — 140
19. Hope, Hype, Potential — 149
20. Health — 157
21. Efficiency — 161
22. Potential (Reward) — 167

Part Three: When — 173

23. When – Momentum — 175
24. Workflow — 197
25. Resources — 208
26. The End is the Start — 211

Contact Me — 216

Acknowledgements — 217

I dedicate this book to my best friend, who I am lucky to have met and married. We started dating during the Great Financial Crash and she has proved to be my best investment by far. Meagan, thank you for investing time with me.

I also dedicate this book to my sons, Fred and Monty, who I hope one day will read it and be captured by the same passion I have enjoyed all my life.

To my parents, who were the very definition of soul mates. They were rarely apart in life and even passed away within 22 days of each other. They always allowed me to find my own path and (even though I veered off it a few times) never pressured me into anything I didn't want to do.

To Paddy, Pete and Steve, friends who I mention in this book. Thank you for humouring me on the weekend podcast, for over seven years, even when your enthusiasm has not quite equalled mine.

Finally, to Mr Barry Williams, my A-Level economics teacher, who ignited my passion for investing. Without that fantasy stocks and shares competition you started, I probably would not have transformed my life in so many ways. The ability to inspire, I believe, is the sign of a truly great teacher.

About the Author

Justin Waite's passion for investing was ignited by a fantasy stocks and shares competition at school. A dream job in stockbroking failed to come to pass, and by his mid-20s Justin had drifted through 25 different low-paid jobs – from serving customers in Marks & Spencer, to picking melons on a Moshav in Israel. In 1999 he lost what little money he had during the dotcom bubble. He eventually managed to land a job in radio, which provided him with enough money to start investing again. During the Global Financial Crisis he lost his job and nearly all his money as the markets collapsed.

Having no luck getting employed, Justin realised his only hope was to become a better investor. From 2009 to 2021, Justin experienced 12 consecutive years of positive gains, with his investment returns totalling over 9,000% at the peak of the bull market – achieving financial independence. The rigours of a bear market helped him refine his methods further, leading to his development of a strategy that works in all types of markets – which he shares in his new book.

Preface: aka The Cheat Sheet

"You get recessions, you have stock market declines. If you don't understand that's going to happen, then you're not ready, you won't do well in the markets."
—**Peter Lynch**

Before you begin

This book will hopefully provide you with a lot of valuable information that will help you become a better investor in a short space of time, even if you only stick to some of the rules.

However, I am aware that it's difficult to remember an entire book or all of the principles within it after just one read. So here's a quick cheat sheet for you on my three-step strategy for lasting stock market success.

✓ What – fundamental analysis

Look to invest in improving businesses that are growing and of good value. By improving I mean the figures, not the management's vision or your perception.

✓ When – technical analysis

Never buy a company in a downtrend, regardless of the fundamentals. Momentum is a powerful force in both directions. A rising share price attracts buyers, a falling share price attracts sellers.

 – portfolio management

Portfolio management is the most important part of investing that is very rarely referred to. Firstly, a low-cost, well-diversified fund should be the backbone to your portfolio. You should invest a regular amount into this fund, preferably on a monthly basis.

When it comes to investing in individual companies, make any new investment *small*. Focus on the risk first, not the reward. That way, if it goes wrong, you are prepared and your loss will be small. So put a stop-loss at 20% below your buy price. This limits your risk.

There will be plenty of time to average up on any extraordinary winners. By doing this your portfolio value will be leveraged towards your winners, not your losers.

Why microcaps?

It's probably worth me pointing out what microcaps are and why I focus on them. But before I do this, I want to stress that **the principles in this book can be applied to any-sized business in any geography**. The strategy I outline was created to simply find quality businesses that are growing, possess good value, and show decent investment potential. They can be found in lots of places. This book also looks at the best time to invest in these businesses and how to manage your investments.

I will provide more detail on this later, but I define a microcap as a UK publicly listed company that has a market capitalisation below £100m.

The reason I focus on microcaps is because it's an area of the market that can produce *outstanding* outsized results. Simplistically it's because smaller businesses that are flourishing can scale at a quicker rate than bigger businesses.

This is also backed up by statistics. Every year I look at the companies whose share prices have outperformed over the last three to five years. I choose this time period because some companies can perform well for 12 months but underperform afterwards. So I aim to find companies that have achieved a sustained rise in their share price, then analyse the traits that led to this performance. The results of my analysis consistently show that 60% of the best-performing businesses start their rise when their market capitalisation is below £100m.

Later in the book I will also look at the traits of ten companies that achieved a minimum return of 1,000% in less than ten years. All these companies started their journey when their valuation was below a £100m market capitalisation. However, I would like to reiterate: the principles I use in this book can be applied to any company, in any country.

If you can absorb these principles after one read of this book, and have the discipline to execute them, you will make money. If, after reading this book, you think you need more help, then you should consider joining my investment club. I repeat these lessons on a live weekly webinar and show you how I put them into practice.

The website also has the UK's first and only MicroCap League, which is a system that ranks companies on the metrics that count when it comes to moving the share prices of small businesses. In short, it's a list of over 100 companies with the best risk/reward profile. Among this list are undoubtedly some big future winners.

If you would like to become a member of the SharePickers Investment Club visit www.sharepickers.com. Because you bought my book you qualify for a 25% discount.

Please be assured: you don't need the website to benefit from the book. I reveal all the principles you need here to invest your way to financial freedom. But if you benefit from the book, I think you'll get a lot from the site too.

Introduction

"The first rule of investment is: don't lose money. The second rule of investment is: don't forget the first rule."
—**Warren Buffett**

Put your money where your book is

I have read lots of investment books over the years and realised not many of them have been written by private investors. There's a good reason for this. Most private investors do not make money investing in individual companies in the stock market.

I also realised that even books written by people working in the industry – 'experts', as they like to be known – very rarely tell you whether they've actually made any money.

They will talk a good game, presenting strategies and stats on how to find winners, but not tell you if they have made any real money themselves. In any industry or profession, the only thing that counts is your track record.

Would you hire a business consultant who has never run a successful business? Or a social media marketing expert who says they can boost your social media presence but, when you check theirs, has fewer followers than you?

When it comes to investing, the return on the money you've invested is the proof of the pudding. So if you ever come across some self-proclaimed expert on social media bigging up a certain stock, ask them, "What's your return over the last ten years?"

Here's mine.

From November 2009 to the time of writing (February 2024), my total return has been 4,620% – and this is after a recent bear market.

During the peak of the bull market, I achieved a return of 9,036%. I started with £30,115 in my ISA in 2009 (which was supposed to have been a mortgage deposit – more on that later) and on 1 May 2021 that value hit a peak of £2,751,467.01p.

I paid my mortgage off in 2020 and still have a seven-figure ISA account (even though I've taken a big hit in the recent bear market).

I am not pointing out my financial achievements to boast. I state this to show you, as a private investor, that I have the relevant experience in order to write a book on investing that will genuinely help people like me: private investors.

I would also like to point out that I have no special qualifications. I did not work in finance or as an accountant. I have previously worked at radio stations and am entirely self-taught. If I can achieve these types of returns, you can too.

The other reason I wrote this book is because I have made money every year, from 2009 to 2024, *apart* from in 2022. Of the knowledge I have accumulated over the last 25 years, I'd say 50% of it was acquired during the 2022–24 bear market (the definition of a bear market is when the price of an index drops 20% or more from its high). The AIM All-Share Index, which features most small and microcap companies, hit a peak on 6 September 2021 – then dropped by 20% by 21 February 2022. This index remained in a bear market until 20 May 2024, when it temporarily entered a bull, a 20% rise from a recent low. However, this bull market lasted only ten trading days – and, since 20 May, has therefore technically fallen back into a bear market.

I have invested through four bear markets: the Dotcom Bubble, the Great Financial Crash, the Covid Dash for Cash Crash and the recent bear market, which lasted over 700 days and saw the AIM All-Share index drop 49%. Remember, this is an entire index, so this drop includes the best performers too. Some companies went down 80% or more – or went bust.

This book uses everything I have learnt in both good times and bad to build a strategy that uses three basic principles to help you avoid losing money, in *all* types of market.

Introduction

What, When, How

These principles will help you find **WHAT** to invest into, **WHEN** to invest and **HOW** to avoid losing money in the stock market. You're probably thinking, 'But I want to make money in the stock market! This book's title is *How to Become a Microcap Millionaire*!'

I know, most private investors think only about making money – it's also why most of them lose it. They don't think, *how much am I going to lose?* Or, *what happens if this investment goes wrong?*

That is why they lose money.

Every investor who consistently loses money – who ultimately gets taken out of the game – is an investor who has focused too much on reward. If you only focus on potential reward, you risk too much. You think, 'If I put lots more money into this, I will *make* a lot more money.'

This is greed. Greed can lead to ruin.

The fact is, private investors rarely focus on risk first. Yet if you can control risk to the point where, if the worst-case scenario happens, it has little impact on your portfolio, **you have cracked the hardest part of investing**.

So the first step in *How to Become a Microcap Millionaire* is to stop losing money. If you then compound this by maximising the gains on your winning investments, your return will be way better than the average investor and many market 'experts'.

You may have heard that investing is all about risk management. This is partly true – but it's only half of the equation. Private investors, generally, lose money for two reasons.

1. They go too big on the wrong stocks and hold on to these losers too long.
2. They sell any winners too early.

So investing is about risk *and* reward management. This is what this book will help you with, in three steps. Well, OK, it's not just three simple steps; I used that for a catchy subtitle. There's a bit more to it, as making money in the stock market is not easy. If it was, everyone would be doing it.

However, I will make it as simple as possible and there *are* three basic steps (with a few additional shuffles) to follow.

1.
It's All About Me (Well, This Chapter Is)

"Experience is what you get while looking for something else."
—Federico Fellini

A reason to be

In life you have to have something that motivates you. Something to get up for in the morning. Something you look forward to. A reason to be. For me, this is the stock market.

For the last 20 years I can probably count on one finger the number of times I have woken up later than 7am.

Monday to Friday, at 7am, companies listed on the stock market release significant news. This is one hour before the market opens for trading.

You never really know what news will emerge at 7am. For investors it's a time filled with expectation. Ideally 7am delivers good news about a company you hold. What you don't want is news that will crater the share price of a company you hold.

If there's no news released about a company you hold, there's plenty of news to scan through which could present you with a new investment opportunity.

It's like the start of a Formula One race – but one with hundreds of cars involved. At 7am you find out whether any of your cars have been allocated a good starting position on the grid.

At 8am the lights turn green and the cars are off.

The market comes to life, with millions and millions of pounds flowing into and out of companies, sending their share prices up and down. It's almost a living breathing entity, an electronic monster whose skin glitters green and red with emotion.

The difference between this race and Formula One is that there's not one winner. The object of the game is to get your cars around the course in a decent time and not to crash off the track. If they can do this, they are making progress. If they can slowly improve their race times over forthcoming weeks, months and years without crashing, you are winning.

This race is re-run every morning from Monday to Friday around 250 days a year.

This gets me out of bed in the morning.

I can pinpoint, to the day, when my passion for investing was ignited. It happened at the age of 16 during an A-Level economics lesson. The lesson itself was boring. Lots of stuff about supply and demand, with accompanying yawn-worthy charts.

However, about 20 minutes before the end of the hour-long lesson, my teacher Mr Barry Williams announced, "We are going to start a fantasy stocks and shares competition."

Finally, my ears pricked up with interest.

"Grab your stuff, we are going to the library", Mr Williams declared.

I don't know what I expected but I can't say I was overcome with excitement when Mr Williams pointed to a wrinkled copy of yesterday's *Financial Times*.

"In this newspaper there's a list of companies listed on the stock market. Your job is to pick one to invest £1,000 into."

"Where do we get £1,000 from, sir?" I asked, thinking I'd just keep the cash.

"It's not real money, Waite! It's a fantasy game. You pick a company to invest your £1,000 into and we check the share price every week to see who makes the most money. At the end of the term the person with the most money wins and will get a prize."

"Will it be the £1,000, sir?" I asked, getting interested again.

"No!" came the reply.

Well, at least it got us out of the classroom for 30 minutes every week.

So we all stared at this huge list of company names with columns of unintelligible numbers next to them, wondering where to start. This was 1986, so the internet had not been invented. The closest we had to dynamic moving share prices was Teletext.

Teletext was on the TV and was basically a televised, coloured version of the *Financial Times* stock price pages with fewer figures. Companies were listed alphabetically in chunks from A–H, I–P and Q–Z.

There were about 20 pages for every section and you had no control over the pages. So if you missed your company's share price, you had to wait another 10–15 minutes for it to appear again.

If you'd told me beforehand that this odd activity of staring at a seemingly endless list of text with numbers would have had any passing interest for me, I'd have looked at you like you were growing a radish out of your nose.

But I became well and truly hooked.

I couldn't explain it, but the pleasure I got from seeing my company's share price going up was only matched with an opposite but more intense feeling of pain when it went down.

I remember sitting for ages staring at these boring Teletext pages, wondering where my share price would be next time my page came around.

Incidentally, this is why I have set up the website Champion Investor (www.championinvestor.co.uk). It's a fantasy stocks and shares competition that is free to play, and which I hope will inspire people to learn about investing. If you haven't tried it, give it a go. Hopefully it's better than Teletext!

One step forward, two steps back

I started investing with real money just before the dotcom bubble burst.

I couldn't believe how easy it was to make money. The whole market was rising but the real opportunities were small companies who changed their name by adding *.com* at the end.

It didn't matter what the company did (if they did anything), whether it generated revenue or had cash, as soon as they changed their name, their share price would at least double. The internet was the future. It promised to deliver all manner of riches to companies prepared to embrace it.

The thing is, as a new investor, you don't realise when you are in a bubble.

Even if there are sufficient signs to acknowledge it, you refuse to believe it. I didn't particularly care why my shares were going up, they just were. If it was because of a bubble, let the bubble keep growing.

I was doing so well I started taking bigger risks, putting more money into individual companies – believing it was impossible to lose money.

Then the bubble popped.

I ended up losing all the money I'd initially invested and more. To this day, I still can't believe how I achieved this.

Lesson one: making money in the stock market is NOT easy.

If it was, everyone would be doing it – and when most people are doing it, you're either at the top of the market or in a bubble.

After the dotcom bubble popped, I dabbled in the stock market on and off for years but I didn't really have any spare money to invest. I was floating from job to job trying to find something I wanted to do.

By the time I was 25 I had worked in 25 different jobs, from insurance salesman in South Wales, to a melon picker on a Moshav in Israel.

At one point I worked in a Marks & Spencer sandwich shop in the City of London. I would often serve stockbrokers fresh off the trading floor in their striped blazers, envious of the careers they had.

I used to buy a *Financial Times* every day, read it on the Tube on the way to work, then read a book about investing on the way home (to my overcrowded shared house).

My dream was to become a wizard

One of the first books I bought was *Stock Market Wizards: Interviews with America's Top Stock Traders* by Jack D. Schwager. I so wanted to be a stock market wizard. When I got home, I used to pull the stock pages out of the *Financial Times* and underline the companies I dreamed of investing in.

I was on a low wage and didn't even have regular hours. I could barely afford the *Financial Times* on a daily basis. Being a stockbroker or a top investor was my dream job. I applied for a few jobs in the City of London but had no proper qualifications and my mental maths wasn't strong.

I always remember applying for a position with an institution at the London Stock Exchange, which I think was an assistant to a stockjobber. A cockney-sounding bloke interviewed me over the phone and just gave me a series of mathematical questions to answer. Things like, "What's 1,083 minus 763?"

I remember being nervous and trying to figure them out. After about ten questions there was a pause. Then the bloke said, "You got three out of ten correct. Sorry, that's not good enough."

As the phone went down, I just figured I wasn't suited to my dream job. So I decided to apply for a place on a degree course in Business Information Systems at the University of Wales, Cardiff. I saw this as a backward step, as I'd spent many years wasting my time swapping one low-paid job for another in the hope of landing some position that I could call a career. It hadn't happened. My mother and father had said I should go to university after A-Levels but I had resisted. They had been right, I had been wrong.

I was accepted at the University of Wales, Cardiff, so with a heavy heart I packed up my bags intending to leave London for Cardiff the next day. I remember looking at the pile of *FT*s sitting on my desk. There must have been two years' worth of stock pages, all neatly laid on top of each other.

I can't quite remember the system I had, but I remember it involved different highlighter pens and a ruler, with copious notes on a pad. I have no idea what colour represented what, but I'd highlighted thousands of stocks over the two years, dreaming it was the way to become a market wizard.

Finally but reluctantly I picked the pile of *FT*s up and dumped them in the bin. At the time I thought, 'That's two years of research down the drain.'

The crash that brought me back

The next morning I was driving down the M4 towards Cardiff to embark on a new chapter of my life. Within 12 months I'd dropped out of my university course to realise my second dream job of being on the radio.

I auditioned for and got the gig of crazy roving reporter on the Red Dragon FM Breakfast Show. This involved me doing stupid stunts or acting like a cheeky chappy around Cardiff for the pleasure of the South Wales listening audience.

More importantly, it provided me with a steady half-decent wage, meaning I got a mortgage for my first flat. It also meant I could start investing again.

My employers were so impressed with my work on Red Dragon FM they said I should apply for the same type of gig on the new *Breakfast Show* on Capital Radio (part of the Capital Group) hosted by Jonny Vaughan. I didn't really want to go back to London as my time there previously had been truly miserable.

I'd left London feeling like a failure, and was happy in Cardiff. Red Dragon FM is where I met friends for life – two of them, Pete and Steve, still appear on a weekend podcast with me (when they can be bothered). Most of the employees were of the same age and our social life was superb. Although this time, if I did land the job in London, the wage would be decent enough for me not to have to live in an overcrowded shared house – and I'd be able to invest some money.

Two years later and the job in London was going well. I had enough money to put a deposit on a flat, plus I was meeting loads of celebs, having a good laugh, making new friends (one of which, Paddy, also appears on the weekend podcast, but even less frequently than Pete and Steve) and attending lots of exciting events.

In 2007, I was offered the chance to host my own breakfast show at a new radio station, Xfm, back in Cardiff. My co-hosts would be Pete and Steve. It was the perfect gig. Getting paid to have a laugh on air with two of your mates. Life couldn't get any better. I jumped at the chance. Not only did I really like Cardiff, but my wage would also be increased.

I handed in my notice in London, sold my flat at the height of the property market, and travelled back to my old flat in Cardiff. This time, leaving London I felt like I'd made it. I had money and was about to embark on a new exciting career in my favourite city.

Then the Great Financial Crash happened.

My job got pulled before I even got in the studio. So I had no job.

On the positive side, I had some money from my flat sale and had started dating a lovely girl by the name of Meagan, who lived in Essex. Meagan would travel down to Cardiff on a regular basis in her little Peugeot 206, and we'd spend many a lovely night out in Cardiff Bay. Everything was good – apart from me being unemployed.

I started working with Ruth Jones on BBC Radio Wales but only on a temporary basis, so the money I was earning was not enough to cover my mortgage. Meagan and I got on so well she soon became pregnant. We decided to let out my flat and rent a house. The rent from my flat didn't cover the house rent but I did have a deposit for a mortgage. All I needed to do was get a decent job to get a mortgage to buy a house.

This wasn't as easy as it sounded. People were being laid off and banks weren't keen on providing mortgages; in fact, they were going bust and frantically trying to rein in their debt. I applied for loads of jobs, many of which I wouldn't have looked at six months earlier. I remember going for a factory job and getting turned down. I was not in a good place.

Having a lot of time on my hands, I decided the obvious thing to do was to double my mortgage deposit by trading on a spread betting platform.

A fat-fingered disaster

After a few weeks of losing money slowly on a daily basis, one day in September the NASDAQ (US tech indices), which I was long on, dropped by about 9% in one session due to what someone described as a fat finger mistake. I looked this up and apparently a fat finger error was caused by a human inputting the wrong amount of data.

This fat finger cost me £9,000.

I was distraught. It was a big hit mentally and financially. It took me weeks to recover any confidence to get back into the market – but I figured I had to get better.

Nobody was offering me jobs and I had no real prospects, plus I had a baby on the way.

So I decided the lesson to learn here was: *never spread bet again*. The odds of earning money, trading like this, are very slim.

I had to go back to investing. The market had just crashed, so it had to go up at some point – didn't it? I just had to find the right company to invest in.

I reasoned that the banks had taken the brunt of the sell off. So what could be a better recovery play than putting your money into a bank during the banking crisis?

I zeroed in on Lloyds Bank.

The bank rollercoaster

Lloyds was one of the biggest mortgage providers in the UK and my logic was, if Lloyds went bust, the UK was in big trouble.

Not the most bullet proof of strategies – but I saw my opportunity. Lloyds' share price had just dropped by 33% in one day. It *had* to bounce. So I put half of my remaining mortgage deposit money into the bank's shares at about 33p.

The next day the share price dropped by another 31%!

So I decided to do the only sensible thing I thought I could do. I invested the other half of my mortgage deposit into it.

The share price started the day down but ended the day flat. Over the next ten days the share price rose from a low of 22p to 51p. I was in profit!

I thought, 'This is easy! Sod working for a living, I don't need your crappy jobs! *Stuff* your jobs!'

Then over the next few days the share price gradually dropped from 51p to 42p. I was confident it would recover. The next day it dropped by 32%.

Somehow, I figured all was not lost. I still had a mortgaged flat in Cardiff Bay and a couple of grand in my bank account. If a sensible option existed it probably would have been to sell – but nothing I was doing was sensible. I decided to invest the last couple of grand into Lloyds too.

Over the following weeks, the share price hit an all-time low of 18p.

The drop was relentless. It was as if the market was personally trying to punish me for my stupidity and vulnerability.

By now I was regularly having sleepless nights. Waking up in cold sweats, dreaming that the government was going to nationalise the bank. I was a mental wreck.

Nationalisation was not a far-fetched nightmare. It was happening. The government had already done it with Northern Rock and Bradford & Bingley. This meant the value of the shares went to zero. The government also took an 83% stake in RBS.

Could Lloyds be next?

When I was getting up in the early hours of the morning, I was smoking heavily and eating lots of rubbish. My waistline was fast gaining the pounds that my portfolio was losing.

Why had I ever left Capital Radio? I had had a safe job there. I was now 40, with no job, a baby on the way, renting a house I couldn't afford and losing money quickly.

I never envisaged myself as being a skint, fat, washed-up failure at 40.

I did think about selling Lloyds but I never went through with it because I was sitting on a loss. I didn't want to reveal this to Meagan; our relationship was already suffering, largely down to my mood.

Then one day I reluctantly woke up after a restless night feeling exhausted, not looking forward to another mentally draining day watching the Lloyds share price drop. To my surprise the share price started steadily rising. This continued for a few sessions.

I didn't want to get my hopes up, as I'd experienced this before only for it to fall by over 50% in a few sessions. I was still tempted to pull all my money out at a small loss – but part of me was determined to get my money back. I'd suffered enough. I needed to get something right to prevent me from being an unmitigated failure. I had earned the right to a profit, hadn't I?

Within a few months the share price hit 70p and I decided to exit. I more than doubled my money but vowed I would never, ever take that kind of risk again.

And I didn't. I changed my ways so thoroughly that from the Great Financial Crash of 2009 to 2021, I achieved an 8,400% return on my money. I will show you exactly how I did it – and how you can do likewise – in the pages ahead.

But I still experienced losses. In fact, in the bear market of 2021 to 2024 my portfolio lost nearly half its value. Which means, I am still up over 4,000% on my initial investment since 2009 – but mad as hell I didn't have a strategy for a bear market.

Now I do. Soon you will too.

2.
It's a Different Animal

> "The Chinese do not have a word for crisis. What they do have, however, is a two-word idiom: crisis equals danger and opportunity."
> —**Bennett Goodspeed**

If you're not evolving, your portfolio will die

I am not a huge fan of football and have only taken an interest in it in the last few years. This is because my youngest son, Monty, has been inspired by his grandad to become a Spurs fan. At the start of the 2023 season there was a resurgence of enthusiasm at Tottenham due to their new manager favouring an exciting attacking game.

Of the first eight games that season, Spurs drew one and won seven. I remember going to watch a game where they beat Liverpool 2 – 1. After the game an enthusiastic fan and his son (who was around seven years of age) bounded past me on the way to the exit. The dad shouted, "We're gonna win the f****** league, son!". His son smiled at his dad proudly.

As the season unfolded, Spurs' winning record started to unravel. Apparently the problem was their defence. Yes, they could score goals – but good opposition teams could too.

The reason for this story is to explain why my strategy has evolved since the bull market. Bull markets usually last around five to seven years but the most recent one lasted for over ten. This was a bull market on steroids, fuelled by the biggest producers of financial stimulus on the planet, the central banks. From March 2009 to March 2022 UK interest rates (and others around the world) didn't get above 0.5%. In March 2020 they went down to 0.1%.

To boost the effect of this turbocharged high, central banks also embarked on a programme of quantitative easing (QE) or bond buying. This inflated their prices, meaning their yields were kept low.

This was the longest period of low interest rates ever. Ever!

Borrowing money was easy because it was nearly free. This was the same for businesses and consumers alike. There was no point putting money into a savings account or bonds because you would get little to no return. Money was being borrowed and spent. If you wanted a return on your money the only game in town was the stock market. Hence the massive money inflow.

The stock market was rallying hard and the hardest-rallying vehicles were the high-risk/reward assets from crypto to hype stocks. The higher the risk and potential reward, the more money piled into them. These were companies short on fundamentals but long on story. Their stories promised all kinds of rewards. All they needed was the funding to get there – and raising funds was easy.

The best strategy to adopt in this market was to go long on the hype, or so I thought.

In August 2021 inflation, barely mentioned over the last ten years, hit 3.2%, above the central bank's 2% target. This sparked rumours of interest rate hikes. On 6 September 2021, the market hit a top, started wobbling and stuttering – wondering where the next financial fix would come from.

At the end 2021 the Bank of England stopped QE. In February 2022, central banks raised interest rates. They went from 0.1% on 19 March 2020 to 5.25% by August 2023. Money was no longer free to borrow and savers could park their money in a bank and get a decent safe return. Massive money outflows from the market started to happen.

What has this got to do with Spurs?

If you are playing against a team with a weak attack and defence, there's a good chance you will beat them if your team's offensive strategy is good. You do not need a strong defence.

This was like the market from 2009 to 2021. This was not a normal market. Everything rose. I would be surprised if we ever see interest rates that low for so long.

If your team is playing a good team **you need to have both a decent attack and defence**. If you want to be a good investor you have to have a strategy for both a bull and bear market. Spurs have since focussed on their defence. A good coach and good investor realises their strategy is only as good as its weakest point. If you can only beat teams with a weak attack and defence, you are never going to win the league. The best teams have strength in both attack and defence.

To become a really good investor you have to evolve and find the best strategy. If this strategy is only suited to a certain environment it isn't the best strategy.

As my high-risk/reward strategy started to fail in the bear market, I was determined to find a better way. I realised that not all stocks were selling off. There were businesses not only bucking the trend but thriving. These stocks were not fuelled by hope. They were fuelled by specific strong fundamentals.

I have since built a system around these fundamentals, called the MicroCap League. The top five companies in this league outperformed the AIM All-Share Index during the bear market by 185%.

This is why I love investing, it's a game of constant learning. And what you learn, you can put into action – and reap the benefits. As we'll soon see.

3.
What Prevents Most People from Becoming Exceptional Investors?

"Successful investors are disciplined. Their investment decisions are not driven by greed, fear, and emotions."
—**Anon**

There are two qualities a person needs to become a successful investor: a willingness to work and discipline.

Work

If you think you can make money picking individual companies in the stock market without putting some effort in, you might as well stop reading now.

If you want to achieve a positive return with little effort your best option is to invest a monthly regular amount in a low-cost, well-diversified fund. I cover this in a later chapter. I believe a fund should be the backbone to every private investor's portfolio. However, if you want to try to achieve a better return than a fund can provide, you need to take on a bit more risk and invest in individual companies. This means spending some time doing some research and learning.

Nothing comes without effort. The most accomplished people in the

3. What Prevents Most People from Becoming Exceptional Investors?

world are not the best just because they have talent alone. And they know it.

> "Talent without working hard is nothing."
> **—Cristiano Ronaldo**

> "I'm convinced that about half of what separates the successful entrepreneurs from the non-successful ones is pure perseverance."
> **—Steve Jobs**

> "Our greatest weakness lies in giving up. The most certain way to succeed is always to try just one more time."
> **—Thomas Edison, inventor**

The good news is: you don't need talent to make money in the stock market. You just need to make some effort. It's like any other profession, activity or hobby – the more you practise it, the better you become.

If you want to consistently make money investing in individual companies, which is not easy, you've got to become good at it. This does not happen overnight. It takes work and time.

It's curious that many new investors think they can start making money as soon as they start investing. This doesn't apply to any other profession. Would you expect to be competing in Wimbledon the same year you start taking tennis lessons?

If you are training to become a brain surgeon, you don't jump in and start operating on a live patient with the hope it will work out. There are years of training – and even when you get to the stage where you find yourself in an operating theatre, with a real living patient, you are supervised.

So this guide will help you learn faster – and, while you are learning, it will keep your mistakes small. Mistakes are important lessons – but it's crucial you keep them small, because a big one can wipe you out and be your last lesson.

To be good at anything, you have to put the work in. Think of how much work you need to do in a regular job to earn £50,000 pa. Think of how much work a self-employed plumber or electrician has to work to earn a similar amount.

Making money is not easy in any walk of life. If you think making money in the stock market is going to be easy, think again. It's like any other profession. If making money in the stock market was easy... everyone would be doing it!

And they're not. Most of them lose.

Multiply your earnings

The difference between a normal job and investing is that, if you become good at investing, there's literally no cap on the amount you can earn. If you are a self-employed plumber, you can earn good money but you are limited to the amount of jobs you can do because there's only a certain amount of hours in the day. To earn more money, you have to work harder.

With investing, if you happen to invest in a super stock, it can return you multiples of your initial investment – and the more you earn from it isn't related to how hard you worked.

I have a passion for investing. It's not work for me. Most evenings you will find me copying and pasting figures from a company's financial report into my website. I will do this 20 or 30 times (not in one night) before I find a company I am excited by.

I love to do this for two reasons:

1. I know I will eventually find a potential winner that can make me money.
2. I love the fact that doing this work will provide rewards.

If you want to make money, you have to do the work. However, if it doesn't feel like work, that's a massive advantage. The learning process can take years, and be painful both mentally and financially.

As you've read, I have paid my dues on both scores. It has taken over 20 years to learn the knowledge I've acquired and written down in this book. The most valuable lessons have been learned in the recent bear market. A good investor has a strategy but will always be learning and evolving.

If Warren Buffett's investment style had not evolved over time, he wouldn't be half as successful as he is today. As Buffett matured, he began to see limitations in his mentor Benjamin Graham's value investing approach. He realised "cigar butt" businesses (stocks at prices far below their intrinsic value, going cheap but with one last puff of profit) were flawed.

He started investing in quality businesses with strong competitive advantages, robust financial performance, and capable management. Businesses he understood and could foresee performing well in the future.

Hence his famous quote, "It's far better to buy a wonderful company at a fair price than a fair company at a wonderful price."

That is why this guide will help you. It will take a lot of pain out of the all-important learning process. I say "a lot" because you will experience setbacks and losses that will not be easy to accept – but they are part of the process.

When an investment goes wrong it has the very opposite effect of what you wanted to achieve. You lose money rather than make it. And it's painful. This emotional pain is needed and should serve as a lesson to take on board, build into your evolving strategy and help you become a better investor.

There will be times when you'll be tempted to go off-piste and invest in companies that seem to have amazing upside. Sometimes you will be right, sometimes you will be wrong – but hopefully if you stick by the HOW (portfolio management) part of this guide, you won't take too big a hit.

Avoid these two mistakes

I want this to sink in. Most private investors lose money for two reasons:

1. They go too big on the wrong stocks and hold on to these losers too long.
2. They sell their winners too early.

This is a double hit to your portfolio as an excellent winner can transform your portfolio value but selling too early means you won't get this benefit – and holding on to outsized losers will compound this issue.

This guide sets out a strategy that is about improving your consistency when making investments. There will be big winners you will miss out on but you will also avoid big losers. In doing this your returns should be positive and consistent.

It's important to remember: if you keep your losers small, they will not detract from your winners.

Going for big high-risk/reward stocks can lead to the boom and bust that I experienced in the Dot Com bubble. By achieving consistency you will be a lot better than the average retail investor.

More than 70% of retail investors lose money in the stock market. If you follow this guide, you will be far better than the average. I want to repeat this several times, so you remember it. Private investors lose money for two reasons:

1. They go too big on the wrong stocks and hold on to these losers too long.
2. They sell their winners too early.

This guide will show you HOW to avoid these issues plus it will help you find WHAT companies to invest in and WHEN to invest in them.

This guide has been created to help you generate positive returns investing in the stock market regardless of market conditions.

In fact, this strategy has been significantly improved because of the 2021-23 bear market. As I mentioned earlier, I gave up nearly half the gains I made from 2009-21 between 2021-22. Think about this. It took me 11 years to make a decent amount of money in the bull market and within a year the bear market took almost half of it off me.

A robust strategy *has* to perform in both bull and bear markets – but, make no bones about it, making money in a bear market can be very hard. That is when the real lessons are learned.

If you stick to this guide, you *will* make money in the stock market. But a few words of warning. You will probably *not* stick to the lessons in this guide. I know because, at times, I have veered off the path. It takes practice to stick to a strategy. It has to become a habit – and forming a new habit takes time. You have to break old bad habits first.

The reason most investors hold on to their losers too long or sell their winners too early is not so much about stock selection, it's about something that prevents most private investors from becoming exceptional.

Discipline

The hardest part about investing is not learning to read financial reports, balance sheets or charts. It's your emotions. Anyone can learn to read financial reports, balance sheets and charts. But not everyone can control their emotions.

Discipline is what separates good investors from poor ones.

As Warren Buffett said, "Successful investing takes time, discipline and patience. No matter how great the talent or effort, some things just take time: You can't produce a baby in one month by getting nine women pregnant."

You can memorise this guide but unless you have **discipline** you will not be able to stick to it. I know because I have failed several times to stick to my own rules. I will research a company then add all its financial data to my website. The colour-coded scoring system blatantly informs me the company isn't a decent investment opportunity. It may come down to lack of growth, value or momentum... but I will invest anyway.

No strategies work without the discipline to stick to them. Lack of discipline will cause you to succumb to FOMO (fear of missing out) and confirmation bias – and therefore lead to **underperformance**.

Make financial investments – not emotional ones

Fear of missing out will cause you to chase stocks and buy them just because they are rising. You'll think they will not stop going up. Although they tend to, as soon as you buy them.

You will invest in these companies regardless of how good the business is. You will overpay for overvalued companies, with little growth or potential just because you don't want to miss out on the rise in the share price.

In many cases, by the time you give into this emotion and invest, the company is likely to be a poor investment choice as the value is already beyond its potential. Then when the share price starts dropping and you find yourself sitting on a loss, you will not sell it because you are emotionally invested in the company.

You didn't invest because the company's growth and valuation was compelling, you invested because you didn't want to miss out on the rise.

This is an emotional investment, not a financial one.

Figures are fact

If you base your investment strategy on financial metrics, there are clear-cut reasons to invest or not, to hold or to sell. When using financial metrics, you invest because a company has growth, is of good value and should be valued higher. If the company releases news that exceeds current growth estimates, then the value should be higher. If they release news that comes in below assumed growth metrics, then the potential valuation should be reduced and you *have* to get out.

It's very clinical.

If you are emotionally invested in a company, you are just weighing up what you *think* about a company. This is not reality. It's an opinion based on your emotions. In short, it's a delusion.

Your emotions can change on a daily basis, and can be unrelated to what's actually happening with a company's operations. Knowing when to sell will also be based on your emotions – and this is where **loss aversion** comes into play.

It's been proven that the emotional pain of a loss is psychologically twice as powerful as the pleasure of gaining. This means you will continue to hold on to your losses to avoid pain.

This loss aversion compounds itself when it comes to holding on to winners too.

If you randomly pick a winner based on emotion, you will not know why it worked or when to sell either. You are likely to take a small profit rather than a big one. This is because, if you are sitting on a profit and the company's share price undergoes a slight dip, you want to avoid the psychological pain of a loss, so you sell before this occurs.

You will not care that the company's value should be a lot higher, as you are only basing your decisions on what you think the share price should do.

The benefits of letting your winners run, and cutting your losers, truly cascade:

- One truly exceptional investment can change your portfolio value. It can also make you psychologically more positive and put you in the mood to analyse why this investment worked out.
- Taking a small loss allows you to objectively analyse why it went wrong. A big loss getting bigger negatively impacts your mental health and clouds your judgement. You are likely to become stressed and think illogically. You may even make the mistake of doubling down and compounding your loss.

Yes, every now and again emotional investors may pick a winner – but for every one of these winners, the investment road is littered with failed companies who seemingly had a good story. I will highlight some later.

Winning from an emotional pick also has downsides. I have witnessed stock investors sitting on a nice profit but who refuse to lock it in because, in their head, their company is always valued more highly. What they can't see is that the rise was based on hope, hype and potential, which can quickly evaporate. **However, to know when it's evaporating you have to have taken an objective view when buying it in the first place.** Emotional investors haven't done this. They are married to the stock and have to hold it from this day forward, for better or worse, for richer for poorer (and it's normally poorer).

Do not fall in love with a company. There are plenty of opportunities out there – more appear every day as often as share prices move. That means a company's value changes. A good company may not be an opportunity today, but it could be in a month's time. Learning to spot these opportunities is the key.

You will not be right all the time; even the most experienced investors get it wrong. So you will experience losers and winners – but it's crucial to learn lessons from both positive and negative outcomes, because that's what will make you become a better investor.

The combination of holding on to your losers too long and selling your winners too early can have a drastic negative impact on your portfolio's value and mental health. **If you set rules that make sense from a** mathematical perspective to avoid this, you cannot lose money over time.

The key is to keep your losers small and make your winners big. This means your portfolio value will be leveraged towards winners and unleveraged towards your losers.

Confirmation bias

Confirmation bias means you will fall in love with the company and its story. Even when the facts and figures say otherwise.

This obsession will cause you to ignore the bad news even when the market disagrees with you. It's important you don't become emotionally over-invested in companies. They are a vehicle for making money and won't care if you lose your money. Your love (or hate) for them isn't reciprocated.

I have known investors who have held shares of a company for years, expecting it to be the next ten-bagger even when they are down on their investment in high double digits.

They disregard the underperformance of the company and its share price because the story is all that counts to them. They love the story. If this was a relationship, the company would be taken to court for emotional abuse.

These fan investors will make excuses for the underperformance as they regard the company as their lover or their god. They hero worship the potential of the story created in their mind. While the story of a company is important, be careful you do not disregard other more important metrics.

I will cover story stocks later but this type of relationship is common for these types of companies because they only have the story. This is because they are largely pre-revenue or loss making.

I have had heated conversations with some of these investors but it's like trying to explain to a member of a cult that their leader is a fraud. They don't want to hear it. In fact, they can't hear it; they are brainwashed by the fairy tale of the company.

I have seen investors change their profile pictures on social media to a company's logo. This is a major red flag.

Be wary of companies that have a legion of unwavering followers. They constantly post encouraging things about the company into an echo chamber of fans. These fans in turn get even more excited and buy more shares, emotionally binding them further to their fairy tale. The bigger their loss gets, the more they convince each other that the upside is even greater.

I can confirm I was biased

I don't want to pretend I haven't succumbed to confirmation bias. I have on many occasions – and the outcomes were invariably negative.

Here are a couple of examples.

In October 2020, I was on holiday in Turkey and due to a technical glitch couldn't buy or sell shares through my stockbroking app. So I had to call the brokers up. Every day I would call up and place another buy on a company called **Escape Hunt** (now XP Factory). At the time it was around 7.5p. I bought enough shares to become a significant holder. I held over 3% of the total shares in issue.

By April 2021 it was 45p a share. This was a gain of 500%. I would talk about this company constantly on podcasts and on social media. They were rolling out their escape rooms at an excellent pace, which were achieving rave reviews, and their CEO was very proficient. Then they acquired Boom Battle Bar, competitive socialising bars. I thought this was a genius move and continued to rave about them.

Over the next two years, the bear market started to bite and the stock dropped to 10p. I was still singing their praises. I eventually got out at 15p. OK, I doubled my money – but there's a huge difference between 500% and 100%.

I should not have let this happen. Hindsight is a wonderful thing but the chart was in an obvious downtrend, like most other small cap stocks, and I should have locked in a bigger proportion of my profits.

Another company where I suffered confirmation bias was called **Gfinity**. It operated within esports and digital media. I managed to gain over 200% on this company but ended up walking away with a loss because I was convinced about the story and got on well with the CEO who was a nice guy. The CEO was sacked and the company is on the brink of going bust with a current market capitalisation of £1.4m.

Liking the CEO and the company is not a reason to stay invested when operations and the shares are underperforming. **Figures are fact, everything else is opinion.** Its figures weren't improving but I convinced myself it was just a temporary blip.

The last example I want to give is a company called **Polarean (POLX)**. It has cutting-edge technology that can help visualise people's lungs 100,000 times better than current technology. I invested into this company in around March 2019 at approximately 17p a share. By September 2021, it was 106p a share and I hadn't sold one.

The firm applied for FDA approval after two successful phase III trials and brokers gave the chance of success at 90%. On 6 October 2021, Polarean released news entitled, 'Complete Response Letter received from FDA'. This basically meant its submission had been refused. The shares dropped by 65% in one day. It felt like a gut punch from Mike Tyson. My friend Pete, who also held stock, referred to it as "Brown Wednesday".

I didn't sell on that day, essentially because I couldn't. I had over £400k invested and the liquidity wasn't there to offload them. This was a stroke of luck as they did bounce by 100% to 35p over the next few sessions, and this buying pressure created enough liquidity for me to get out. As I had averaged up on this stock, I got out with a small loss – but I had been over 200% up at one point.

On 21 May 2024, Polarean conducted an equity fundraise at 1p a share, a pre-money valuation of £2.15m. Before it had received the Complete Response Letter from the FDA, its market capitalisation had been closer to £200m.

There's a better way

These three examples show the danger of confirmation bias but also taught me there's a better way, which I will explain soon.

Because of these stocks I have come in for a lot of flak from some investors who bought into my energy and enthusiasm. I still get people trolling me on social media about them.

It has taught me to rein in enthusiasm because there will always be people who do not do the research and will just invest on my say so, regardless of when I bought. I fully expected XP Factory to break 50p and head towards 100p. I said so on many occasions. But it didn't. It dropped to 10p. So the people who invested at 40p or more were sitting on a big loss. Is their loss my fault?

The way they attacked me, you would think I had logged into their stockbroking accounts and bought the stock for them. It doesn't matter how much I say, "Do your own research" – there will be people who don't. They just expect to make money off 'tips' from others.

You will never make money following other people's opinions. If I buy a stock at 7.5p and you are buying at 40p, you had better have a good reason for doing so other than 'this guy seems to think they will go to £1'.

Making money in the stock market is not easy. Even very experienced investors get it wrong.

As I said earlier, losses are lessons. If you learn from them, you will become a better investor. However, if you blame the loss on someone else, you fail to learn any lesson as you won't own the mistake.

A good investor accepts responsibility for his own investments, a bad investor blames someone else for them.

Underperformance

Fear of missing out and confirmation bias are the traits of a poor investor. If you want to become a successful investor you must recognise these are real issues. They can be hard to identify. A deluded investor does not know they are deluded. This is why they are deluded.

Fact is more important than opinion. **Numbers** are more important than the narrative.

This is why it's important to have a robust strategy. That is, a strategy that will allow you to better identify the stocks with a higher probability of giving you a positive return. But equally as important is to have the emotional discipline to stick to that strategy.

Without this discipline you are prone to FOMO and confirmation bias, which leads to underperformance. Having a robust strategy doesn't mean you won't miss out on some winners or completely avoid picking losers. But your hit rate in picking winners will improve and your losses will be minimal on the losers.

Reminder

No strategies work without the **discipline** to stick to it.

So discipline is the foundation of any strategy. Remember, without discipline you will be, at best, an average investor. With discipline you can become a great investor.

The markets will test you. But if you have a good strategy backed by discipline, you will make money.

4.
Risk vs Reward – There Are Two Sides to Every Story

"Remember the two benefits of failure. First, if you do fail, you learn what doesn't work; and second, the failure gives you the opportunity to try a new approach."
—**Roger Von Oech**

The point of investing is to achieve a **positive return** on the capital you **risk**. Therefore investing is about... **risk vs reward.**

It's possible, but is it probable?

Investing, like everything else in life, is about probability. As an example, if you wanted to cross a busy road, your desired outcome would probably be to get across the road safely. Your unwanted outcome would be to get hit by a vehicle, weighing 20 times more than you, travelling at 30 mph.

To increase the probability of you achieving your desired outcome, you would use your eyes and ears to make yourself aware of oncoming traffic. You would then cross when there seems to be no vehicles in close proximity.

What would happen if you tried to do the same wearing a blindfold and earplugs? How would this change the probability of you achieving your desired outcome?

This is the same with investing. This book will show you how to increase the probability of you achieving your desired outcome.

The desired outcome with investing is a positive return, which means making a profit. The unwanted outcome is to make a negative return, which means making a loss. By assessing the **risks** and **reward** accurately, you can protect yourself against the risk while not reducing your exposure to the reward.

Therefore, accurately assessing risk and reward increases your chances of achieving a positive return. The ideal scenario is to find potential investments that **possess small risk but with big potential reward**.

So the first job is to assess whether a potential investment possesses a decent enough reward. If there's very little reward on offer there's no point risking your capital.

When I refer to a decent reward investing in small companies, I mean a minimum of 40% over a 12-month period. This may not sound huge but it adds up to over 174% over three years. If you start your investing journey with £10,000 and manage to achieve a return of 40% a year for 20 years, the compounding effect of this means you will have amassed £5.9m.

I am not saying you are going to achieve this, I am just pointing out the power of compounding to achieve spectacular returns. You don't have to find a ten bagger (but it is a possibility with this strategy). You just need to achieve a consistent return for it to pay handsomely.

Once you're assured a potential investment has a decent reward it's essential to find out the risk. The **risk** of achieving the **reward** needs to be thoroughly assessed, as a very big risk could reduce the possible reward to nothing or even a negative. In other words, you'll lose money.

The MicroCap League on SharePickers.com, available to all members, helps assess rewards and the risks associated with achieving them. Companies are scored according to their risk and reward using the metrics, growth, value, health, efficiency, momentum and potential. This means if a company scores high on all these metrics, they not only possess growth but are good value, healthy, efficient, have momentum and are forecast to go on to greater heights. This will in turn help you raise the probability of achieving a positive return.

This book will show you how to do all this yourself.

Getting poor quickly

A lot of small cap investors tend to go for a high-risk/reward strategy because they want to get rich quickly. I don't blame them. If I had a choice between getting rich quickly or slowly, I'd be mad to go for the slow option. However, in taking this approach, there is another possibility: getting poor very quickly. And in fact, high-risk/reward situations are actually telling you that this possibility is a *probability*.

A lot of investors see reward on offer but not risk. Both need to be weighed on all companies. Generally, if a company has a huge broker target price – in other words, professional analysts agree there is room for it to go much higher – it doesn't actually mean the chance of the company achieving it is *probable*. It means the opposite. High-risk/reward strategies possess a potential big reward – but this comes with a big risk. That's why the hypothetical reward is so substantial. And if the big risk plays out, it affects the reward. If it wipes out the money you use to trade, it can affect all future possible rewards, too, by taking you out of the game.

Example

Let's say you have been researching two different companies and can't decide where to put your money. Company A has a broker target price 500% above its current share price and company B's broker says it has 50% upside. Which would you go for?

You'd obviously go for company A as it has 500% upside. However, let's say company A is a pre-revenue biotech stock, the success of which relies on positive clinical trials and a licensing deal with a partner plus commercial rollout of its latest drug. However, company B is a profitable software-as-a-service company, with high recurring revenue.

You have to price in the risk of these companies achieving the reward stated. Let's say the chances of company A achieving this target price is just 10% due to the amount of risk involved in its business model. Whereas the chance of company B achieving its target is 80%.

There's a high probability of company A not achieving its target. In fact, there's a 90% chance. This means if you made ten £1,000 investments in companies with a similar risk/reward profile to company A, you would only be successful on one occasion out of ten. This return would be £1,000 × 500% = £6,000 on the £10,000 you'd invested. So you would have lost £4,000 or 40%.

With company B there's a high probability of you achieving your target price, in fact eight out of ten times you would have increased your investment by 50%. If each of your eight investments became £1,500 that would be £12,000 on the original amount invested, a £2,000 profit or 20%.

If you started with £10,000 and managed to generate 20% returns over 20 years you would end up with £319,480, or 3,095% gain. If you managed to lose 40% a year, your £10,000 after 20 years would be worth 61p.

This is a very simplistic model as it assumes no value at all to the investments that didn't work out. However, it illustrates that you always need to weigh up the risk associated with the reward. Any chance of success below 50% means it's an odds-against chance, i.e. it's possible but not probable. You need to select companies with a probable chance of achieving a decent reward.

Trying to price in the risk for the reward is called a **risk-adjusted outcome.** For example, a pre-clinical biotech company developing a novel medicine that cures a disease with a high unmet medical need will need to test this drug to ensure it's safe and effective. They first have to conduct pre-clinical trials in test tubes (in-vitro) then maybe on an animal (in-vivo). After this they have to conduct three different phases of clinical trials (in humans). Each trial becomes increasingly rigorous, takes more time and costs more money.

Roughly, these are the chances of a drug going from each phase through to commercialisation.

- phase I = 10%
- phase II = 30%
- phase III = 60%
- approval by FDA = 90%.

So if a company is in phase I and the drug they are developing could achieve sales of $1 billion, you have to understand there's only a 10% chance of this. Therefore there's a 10% chance of $1bn or $100m. So if this is a nanocap (market capitalisation sub £20m) there's still some decent upside – but there's a high chance of failure. Aside from the clinical risk, there's the funding risk. If they can't secure the funding, the hope, hype and potential story can't flourish.

Investing is all about probability. If you invest in a high-risk/reward stock, this means the probability of you achieving the big reward is minimal. In fact, it's an odds-against bet. You need to invest in companies where the odds of achieving the reward is probable or odds on.

Many people will say investing is not gambling. Gambling is about risking your capital to achieve a reward. It's the same with investing – but you can achieve far better odds than with gambling. I know this because, in a previous life, while trying to find a career, I was a manager for the bookmaker William Hill.

The Grand National is the most famous horse race in the world, where around 30 horses race over four-and-a-quarter miles jumping 16 fences, 14 of which are jumped twice. Of course, it's hard to pick a winner as there are so many horses and the odds on each horse winning is odds against. (The odds are the return you can expect to get if the horse you bet on is successful.)

If a horse has odds of 10 to 1 this means if you bet £1 on this horse and it wins you would win £10 plus your stake money of £1. This also suggests for every 10 times this horse ran in this particular race, it would be likely to only win it once. So this is a 10% chance of winning or a 90% chance of losing. Over the last 40 years the average odds of the winning horse in the Grand National was 20 to 1 but horses with odds of 100 to 1 have won it. So you might think, why go for a 20-to-1 horse when you could win on a 100-to-1 horse?

You shouldn't go for the high-risk/reward strategy because it's very unlikely to pay off. The high reward tells you this. Here are the stats. In the last 40 years, only one horse with odds of 100 to 1 has won the race; that's a 3% chance of winning. So 97% of the time you would lose your money.

Whereas horses with odds of less than 20 to 1 have won the race 28 times out of 40, a 70% chance. This means you only have a 30% chance of losing compared to 97% if you'd backed 100-to-1 horses.

The big mistake

One of the biggest mistakes private investors make is going too big on high-risk/reward plays. This is why most of them lose money. They tend to believe the high risk means it comes with a high reward. This is a misconception. It means *if* the company is successful it could provide a good reward – *and* that the chances of it happening are slim.

In other words, the chances of achieving this reward are against the odds, i.e. less than 50%. In order to make consistent money investing, you are better off going for a lower reward with greater chances of achieving it, hopefully greater than 50%.

High price targets for stocks are the same as long odds at the horses.

Here's another example. Imagine someone says to you:

> "You have ten footballs and you have to kick them into the back of the net against one of two goalies. The first goalie is Liverpool goalkeeper Alisson Becker, regarded as one of the best in the world, and your chances of beating him are about 1 in 10. Or you can pick your mate Dave, who is out of shape, short sighted and has never really played football let alone been a goalie. Your chances of scoring against him are 8 out of 10. I will give you double the money for every goal you score against Becker as you score against Dave. So you will get £10 for every goal scored against Dave, £20 against Alisson."

Which would you pick?

Even if you do three times as well as the odds suggest against Becker, you will only win £60. You only have to get seven past Dave, less than the odds suggest, to achieve a better return.

So even though the reward is less, you are more likely to achieve it. This is the same with investing. Putting all your money into high-risk/reward stocks is a false economy as you are more likely to lose money than make it.

Don't get me wrong. I am not saying to completely avoid these high-risk/reward plays. They can be portfolio makers, if you manage the risk correctly, but portfolio breakers if you don't. But when you consider that most longer-term successful stock market performers not only generate revenue and profits but are growing, you can start to wonder whether these high-risk/reward plays are even worth it.

5.
What, When, How and Where

"An investment in knowledge pays the best interest."
—Benjamin Franklin

What, **when** and **how** can be seen as three levels of security that will help you increase the probability of achieving a positive return by protecting you against the **risk** while exposing you to the **reward** of investments.

Security of your capital (money) is paramount because if you lose your capital you can no longer invest. Most private investors lose money when investing in individual companies because they make three basic mistakes that can be corrected relatively easily with some discipline. If you can avoid these three reasons why private investors lose money, there are only two other possible outcomes: breakeven or profit.

WHAT to buy – first level of security

The first level of security – deciding what to buy – is about fundamental research. This involves looking at companies' income statements, balance sheets and cash flow statements, analysing companies for growth, value, health, efficiency and potential.

WHEN to buy – second level of security

The second level of security – determining when to buy – involves **technical analysis**: looking at charts to assess whether a company's share price is experiencing net supply or net demand. This will affect whether a company's share price has downward momentum or upward momentum. Momentum is a very powerful force. Just avoiding downtrends can help your investment performance significantly.

HOW to buy – third level of security

The third level of security – choosing how to buy – involves portfolio management, one of the most important aspects of investing very rarely referred to. How you manage your portfolio is the difference between making money and losing it. If you manage your portfolio properly you do not need to be right even half the time.

The foundation of the strategy: discipline

Making rules that make sense is the easy part. Having the discipline to stick to these rules is the hard part. As I've mentioned previously, discipline is what separates average investors from great ones. If you do not have the mental fortitude to stick to your rules, you may as well not have any rules.

Where to buy

Before I get into the what, when, how of investing I want to quickly cover the **where**.

If you are a UK taxpayer and not holding your shares in a stocks and shares ISA, you are giving up even more of your hard-earned income to the taxman/woman. I say even more because the taxman/woman will tax you at every opportunity they get. They are more creative than the mafia when it comes to extracting cash from people.

If you earn a wage, that is taxed. If you drive to work, you probably paid VAT on your car purchase, you pay duty on the fuel you put into it and you pay road tax. When you buy a house you have to pay stamp duty. If you saved money in the bank to afford a deposit for the house, you will have to pay tax on the interest, even though your wage was already taxed and you paid national insurance on it.

You also pay stamp duty when you buy and sell shares. If you make a capital gain on those shares above £3,000 (at the time of writing) you have to pay capital gains tax, even though the money you probably used for that purchase was already taxed.

Not content with taxing you while you are living, if you've done well throughout your life and made some prudent decisions with your hard-earned money, they will be going through your pockets long after you've no need for the trousers (although there is a work around here, covered later).

This is why it is essential, if you have not done it, to set up a **stocks and shares ISA**. It is pretty much exactly the same as a normal stocks and shares trading account but it is a tax-efficient investment account. At the time of writing you can deposit up to £20,000 every tax year and any gain you make is out of the grasp of the tax people. You pay no income or capital gains tax on your investments.

So it doesn't matter how much profit you make on your shares, it is not taxed. Even if you strike lucky and make a gazillion pounds of profits or more, it won't be taxed. However, you can only add a maximum of £20,000 to this account every tax year. And you can't go back in time. So if you have investments sitting in a non-ISA account, £20,000 is the maximum you can move across in any financial year (6 April to 5 April). For many years this allowance was increased on an annual basis but it has stayed at £20,000 since 2017. Probably because the taxman/woman feels they were missing out on income here.

If you're not in the UK, there are probably similar tax-advantageous ways of trading where you are – a quick search online will pay off in the long run.

The Alternative Investment Market (AIM)

The Alternative Investment Market is a small part of the London Stock Exchange (LSE). It exists to help smaller or start-up companies access capital from the market. Therefore to encourage investment into these businesses extra incentives are offered to investors.

Certain AIM shares qualify for **business property relief**. This means that, after being held for two years, the value of any qualifying AIM shares in your ISA will be excluded from your inheritance tax calculation. You must have held these shares for at least two years and still be holding them on your death for them to qualify for exemption. Investing in AIM shares via an ISA means that you benefit from tax breaks and your beneficiaries can receive 100% of the value.

Of course, it's worth pointing out here: you still have to pick quality businesses because tax relief on a worthless stock is irrelevant. AIM tends to come in for a lot of negative press, because it has its fair share of dross. Start-up companies are quite risky and therefore are more likely to go bust than more mature businesses. When a company on AIM goes bust it attracts more attention than a business doing well. There are also a fair number of AIM companies like oil, gas or resource exploration firms that will never produce anything meaningful in their lifetime apart from more shares at a discount.

However, most of the companies I own are listed on AIM and I believe them to be of good quality. Do not be convinced that only companies of low quality are listed on AIM. Yes, there are plenty of low-quality companies on AIM – but they only exist because low-quality investors put their money into them.

Just a quick note: Some of the new challenger ISA providers that offer low or no fees may have a limited number of companies available on their platform. I have heard one or two fellow investors mention they could not buy certain AIM-listed companies with their provider. So check with these providers to make sure you can invest in the companies you want to. These new providers may be cheap or free to deal – but it seems you only get what you pay for.

Part One:
How

6.
How to Buy: Portfolio Management

"Don't look for the needle in the haystack. Just buy the haystack!"
—**John C. Bogle**

Control the controllables

I have read many investment books over the last 30 years and I find it incredible that none of them deal with **portfolio management**, as it is essential to learn in order to make money – or, more accurately, to not lose money.

It is one of the only controllables in an environment you have no control over.

You have no control over a company's management or operations but you *do* have control on how much you invest in that company. Portfolio management falls within your circle of control and can influence the result, rather than be the result itself.

Having no portfolio management is like trying to build a house without any plans. This is exactly why I want to start with the third level of security: how to buy. Portfolio management is probably the most important part about investing and it is very rarely referred to or adhered to by private investors.

If you do not have a robust portfolio management strategy it's unlikely you will ever make a significant amount of money.

The backbone

Firstly, before I talk about individual companies I want to suggest that a low-cost, well-diversified fund should be the backbone to your portfolio.

What kind of fund?

There are almost as many funds as there are shares. I'm being quite specific here. You want an index fund (or trackers as they're sometimes called). These aim to mirror the performance of benchmarks like the S&P 500 by copying their holdings, so there's no active decision making by fund managers.

Jack Bogle is responsible for popularising the index fund. He started Vanguard in 1975. After analysing the performance of active funds he realised that (on average) active funds underperformed the S&P 500 index, and that the shortfalls were often equal to the cost incurred by fund managers at the time. Remove (or drastically reduce) that cost, copy the index, and you can get above-average performance without analysing a single stock.

Currently Vanguard is the largest provider of mutual funds and the second-largest provider of exchange-traded funds (ETFs) in the world after BlackRock's iShares.

According to Morningstar, as of December 2023 the total amount invested in passive funds was $13.29 trillion, higher than the $13.23 trillion held in actively managed funds. Even Warren Buffett suggests most people should just invest in an S&P 500 tracker.

> "If a statue is ever erected to honour the person who has done the most for American investors, the hands-down choice should be Jack Bogle."

Studies have shown about nine out of ten actively managed funds failed to match the returns of the S&P 500 benchmark over the previous 15 years. Why spend loads of hours looking for individual opportunities when you could just put your money into a low-cost S&P 500 index fund?

This index has returned a historic annualised average return of around 10.26% since its inception in 1957, through to the end of 2023.

In chapter 9, I will explain my choice of funds in detail.

The reason you go looking for individual companies is to achieve a bigger return than 10.26%. I've got there, and this book can get you there. But achieving a bigger return means bigger risk. Knowing that you've secured at least some of the returns of the market no matter what can make those risks more manageable both emotionally and (if things go wrong) financially.

And how much is a backbone?

I have some detailed thoughts on this. Instead of bogging things down here, head over to chapter 9 for my system.

So the **first rule of portfolio management** is: have a backbone. It makes it easier to stand in the storms of the stock market.

Think risk not reward

Alongside your trusty backbone of a fund, you need to get your thinking about your portfolio right.

When it comes to investing in individual companies the following sentence will help you more than you think possible, as long as you can think about it before you make *every* investment. Before any investment, always think: **How much can I lose on this investment?**

Do *not* think: How much can I make on this investment?

If the worst-case scenario happens, and a company you're invested in goes bust, what would your portfolio look like?

I say worst-case scenario (barring a nuclear war) because this is how secure your portfolio should be. Prepare for the worst and anything less than this is not a worry. If you focus on this question – *how much can I lose on this investment?* – you are focusing on the **risk**. Investing is first and foremost about **risk management**.

Only when you get into profit should you be focusing on both the risk and reward. Remember, you are trying to find a winning investment. There can be no certainty any investment will make you money.

This is what most private investors get wrong. They only focus on the reward. They think, 'This investment is going to make me rich. So if I put more money into it, I can only make more money.' When an investment goes wrong, and some inevitably will, they therefore have no plan. This results in them sitting on a big loss they haven't the heart to cut.

Investing is about risk and reward. It's no coincidence that risk comes first in this phrase. You risk your capital in order to attain a reward.

Believe it or not, investing is *not* about winning, **it's about not losing**. It's about avoiding big losses first and then about maximising your winners next.

If you do not lose, the winning (largely) takes care of itself.

So flip your current reasoning and think, 'Which company can provide me with the lowest risk for the best return?' When you start focusing on the risk first, you become a better investor.

So the **second rule of portfolio management** is having this goal in sight: invest in a range of low-risk companies which have meaningful potential. (Later chapters will show how to find these.)

What do I mean by a range?

A good target number is up to 20, and you want these to be in several different industries because sometimes companies move together like sheep. More on this in chapter 11.

You have time to build to that. You only want to buy when a share genuinely passes all the tests we are going to put it through.

Having a range means you are diversified. And that will keep you safe when bad things hit the fan.

Investments will go wrong

You are going to make investment decisions that go wrong.

Even the best artists release songs that don't become a hit. Do they dwell on their failures and say, "That should've been a hit! I am going to spend a load more money on marketing and release that song again! It will be a hit!"?

Top sports people lose games. Do they say to their opponent, "Let's play that again. I should have won that"?

The **third rule of portfolio management** is to not deny when you have made a bad investment decision. It can seriously prevent your development, as well as harming your portfolio.

When you find yourself sitting on a loser, you can choose to do one of two things.

1. You can take a small loss, learn from it, and apply that lesson to your next investment.
2. You can deny you were wrong and let the loss get bigger, or throw more money into your mistake and double down on your loss.

If you choose the former, your portfolio will not be shaped by this loser. In fact, you will gain from it educationally. If you choose the latter, your portfolio will be shaped by your losses and you have not learned anything. **Do not believe a company will give you a positive return until it's in profit.**

The **fourth rule of portfolio management** helps avoid a similar error often made at the time of purchase. You want to be equally convinced of the merit of every share you buy. And that means giving them an equal weight in your portfolio when you buy. Even if you have a sneaky feeling one might do better, always start with the same initial investment.

Why?

Again, it's about risk and reward. There are always uncertainties in investing – even if all the probabilities are matched. And having favourites is a form of sloppiness and ill-discipline that can quickly get out of hand. Let's say you have £10,000 in cash and decide to make two investments. Instead of investing equally, you're convinced one could do better – so you put 70% into that, and 30% into the other. One investment doubles in value and the other halves in value.

Unfortunately you put £7,000 into the company that halved and £3,000 into the company that doubled.

This means your £7,000 is now worth £3,500 and your £3,000 is worth £6,000. So in total you have lost £500 (£3,500 + £6,000 = £9,500).

Before you invest into companies, you might *think* one investment will make you more money than another – but if you conduct the research using the metrics I set out in this guide, *all* your investments will have a high probability of providing you with a positive return. We just can't guarantee that the share prices will all move the way we hope. Some *will* lose. And so we make equal bets. Before I go into this, I am talking about companies you perceive to have similar risk/reward profiles after initial research.

These equal bets are also *small* bets in proportion to our overall portfolio. If you have £10,000 to trade, and three stock ideas, I am not saying you put £3,333 in each. A position should be between 1 and 3% of your portfolio.

Why?

Because the bigger the position, the bigger the loss could be. Even with a 20% stop, 20% of a holding that is 50% of your portfolio is still very painful.

I would never suggest you put £5,000 into one company if your total portfolio value is £10,000. That's half your money. That means it's possible to lose half of your entire portfolio value on one stock. And a 20% stop-loss still means losing 10% of everything. Think risk. Think about the worst-case scenario.

I talk about exposure later but things can go wrong, even in the safest of investments. It doesn't matter what has previously happened in a company before you invest. It only matters after you invest – and you will never be 100% certain it will play out as you expect. So your initial investment should always be small. There's always time to invest more if it starts going in the right direction.

More on this in chapter 10.

Example

Let's take that previous example again. This time you expose yourself equally to both, putting £5,000 in each.

The first investment would be worth £2,500 and the second would be worth £10,000. Meaning you are £2,500 up. That's a 25% return.

Remember, most investors lose money by holding on to their losers too long. So let's say you add a simple rule of selling an investment if it drops by 20% below your initial buy price – a **stop-loss**.

On the first £5,000 you invested, you'd have sold when it was worth £4,000. The second investment doubled to £10,000. So in total you have £14,000.

That's a 40% return on your investments and it's a 60% better return than if you had not cut your loss.

Let's say you also put a stop-loss on your winning stock. You are now

100% up on this but choose to put a stop-loss that will kick in and sell your holding automatically if it drops 20% from this high. This means the minimum reward you will receive will be £8,000 on that investment. You have lost £1,000 on your other investment so in total you have made £2,000, a 20% gain. This is the minimum you can make. Your winning investment could go even higher. If that is the case you just move your stop-loss up and lock in more of a gain.

You are managing your losers and your winners. This is risk and reward management. It's the **fifth rule of portfolio management**: there is nothing benign about neglect. Control losses through position sizing and stop-losses, and secure wins not only by giving them space – but by setting stops to guarantee profits once things move in the right direction.

And, as we'll discuss in chapter 11, you can also add to winners and enjoy more upside.

As with stops set to prevent losses, I like to set them 20% below highs. This ensures that the stop doesn't get hit with the day-to-day froth of price movements, and I can stay along for as much of the ride up as possible.

I share more detail on stop-losses in the next chapter, and more on position sizing in chapter 10.

The pain's too great

Taking a loss is painful and the bigger the loss becomes the more painful it is. I've already covered this in these rules of portfolio management, but I'm aware that many reading this will have invested already – and may well be in possession of a portfolio filled with losing shares going nowhere.

If you're already down over 20%, and the share is just bouncing along the bottom of the barrel, my portfolio management advice just provided won't help you. Something extra is needed.

I would *not* automatically suggest selling if you are sitting on a loss of 20% of more as I have no idea if you stuck to rule number one: start small. If you started small then I would say cut but it also won't matter if you don't as it won't massively affect your overall portfolio value.

If you have gone too big then all you can do is *hope* it rebounds. A reminder: hope is not a proven investment strategy. So to make sure you never get into this situation again, **start small!**

Pain is why most investors hold on to their losers. They become too painful to take. You might think, 'This business will recover, I will wait.' Some will – but you have no guarantee of that. The loss could get bigger and bigger.

What if you do this with all your losers? Your portfolio will get dragged down and leveraged towards your losers. You have to be ruthless. If you apply the 20% stop rule going forward, you do have a guarantee: a guarantee your losers will not get out of control and spoil your overall portfolio performance. This is risk management.

Don't beat yourself up for having a screen of red right now. Many private stock pickers do. But we're going to outperform the average. That's the way to make meaningful money.

Example

Imagine this scenario again. You research two companies but feel one is really going to make you rich. So you invest your entire £10,000 into it. Then it drops by 50%, leaving you with £5,000.

It will be emotionally very hard to sell this stock now. You do not want to lose half your money. If I gave you the opportunity to take a £2,000 loss rather than the £5,000 loss, would you take it?

I think most would. And they'd be right to. And that's why stop-losses are important.

The fact is, you *will* take losses. Would you prefer them to be big or small? (If you want more detail on stops, I walk through everything in the next chapter.)

Emotional balance

In order to manage your portfolio properly you have to **think in terms of risk**, not reward. And that means controlling losses above all. Get that right, and everything flows from it. It's much easier to maintain emotional balance taking small losses, and doing so will allow you to become a better investor. You are preserving emotional capital as much as financial.

And that will help you not succumb to other mistakes of desperation.

Get this right and you are more than half way to becoming a better investor. I say more than half way because all you have to do next is not sell your winners too early. This is a lot easier than taking losses. More on this later.

The rules of portfolio management

1. Put a meaningful amount of your trading capital in a low-cost, diversified fund. This means you're guaranteed to capture a chunk of market performance no matter how the rest of your portfolio does. It takes the pressure off. Everything else is gravy.

2. Aim for 10–20 low-risk companies with meaningful potential. Low-risk is more important than high potential, because high potential is by definition not highly probable. And diversification is your ever-present help in times of trouble.

3. Avoid denial when things go wrong. Cut losses. Learn lessons. Move forward.

4. Make equal bets by giving equal initial weights to your investments. (Obviously, if you have winners over time, they will grow to be greater than this.) And avoid risking everything by keeping those initial positions small – 2–3% of your trading capital.

5. Don't neglect your portfolio. Trim losses, secure wins – stop-losses will do both for you automatically. Set them 20% away. Do not sell your winners – guarantee them by moving stops up as they grow.

Your last line of defence

Ultimately, portfolio management is your last line of defence. The **what** to buy and the **when** to buy, which I cover later, are very important – but they won't protect you.

Threats are many:

- bear markets
- company frauds
- big contract cancellations
- profit warnings
- CEOs unexpectedly resigning
- funding shortfalls
- other unforeseen events.

Only the **how** to buy can protect against these – that is, portfolio management.

I'd like to end with a couple of personal examples of all this in action.

Example

Let's say you put all your money into a company that you are convinced is going to make you a lot of money and everything the CEO says suggests the company should be valued at ten times its current valuation (this does happen on AIM).

Then one day the company releases news that the CEO, the person who has given you the confidence to invest so much in the company, is to stand down immediately. The share price plummets. In my experience, if you get out before the share price drops by 30% you should count yourself lucky.

In the best-case scenario the company gets another CEO within a few months – but without the old CEO, all confidence in the stock is lost. This happened to me with a company called **Destiny Pharma (DEST)**. One day the CEO, who I'd interviewed many times, just stood down, without any explanation. The share price dropped by double digits and continued to drop for weeks.

Fortunately, I had followed one of my rules of portfolio management, and that's not to go too big on an initial investment. So the drop was not too painful.

Be wary of pinning your hopes on a story, especially if the CEO plays a big part in this story or is the one responsible for inflating it. If they step down, the share price will fall significantly. Sometimes the lack of explanation for a CEO stepping down is a godsend. Recently a CEO of a company listed on AIM had to stand down because it was found that he'd been loaning his stock to a third-party company.

Example

I recently invested in a company called **SRT Marine (SRT)** for all the wrong reasons due to lack of discipline. Its most recent set of results (interims or H1) showed no growth and it had also pushed its year-end reporting date out by six months to include big orders that were apparently incoming. I should not have invested on the expectation that these orders would happen. They were by no means guaranteed.

The value was also not compelling on current figures. It was more compelling on forecasted figures, but forecasts are just that. Also, there was absolutely no momentum in the share price at all.

You're probably thinking, *why did you invest?*

I invested on hope, even though hope isn't an investment strategy. The broker had forecast excellent growth from already received orders, and their target price was 300% above its current price.

I focused on the reward before the risk.

The only aspect of this investment I got right was my portfolio management. I only invested 1% of my total portfolio value and put a stop-loss 20% below my buy price.

On Tuesday 23 April 2024, the volume was twice that of the average daily volume and the share price started dropping. After around a 10% drop on that day, my stop-loss kicked in (the share had already fallen 10% from my buy). So I lost 20% of 1% of my total portfolio value (or 0.02%). I kept my loss small.

The share price dropped even further during the day and it ended up 19% down that day at close of trading (29% down from when I had bought). I couldn't understand where the volume was coming from. The company had not released any news.

The next day the share price dropped by another 10% on open.

At 9.48 am the company released news entitled, 'Response to reports in Philippine press', where it stated:

> "SRT notes the recent share price movement and reporting in the Philippine press with regard to the IMEMS fisheries project.
>
> "SRT wishes to clarify that the IMEMS contract was won following a competitive international tender, which has been successfully implemented and is operational. On Monday the Ombudsman confirmed that both SRT and Richard Hurd are cleared, but has recommended further investigation into Simon Tucker and other individuals outside of SRT. The Board is fully supportive of Simon who is now working to clear his name."

So even if you make a mistake on your investments, your portfolio management can save you. Take portfolio management seriously. It's the last line of defence.

CEOs standing down in questionable circumstances may be rare but why not account for a possible risk like this? If you are protected against the worst-case scenario what else can go wrong? The happy answer is: very little. Manage your portfolio!

7.
Stop That Loss

"Maybe you're right 5 or 6 times out of 10. But if your winners go up 4- or 10- or 20-fold, it makes up for the ones where you lost 50%, 75%, or 100%."
—**Peter Lynch**

Stop-losses

Throughout my investment journey I have had an on-off affair with stop-losses but now I swear by them.

First of all, *what is a stop-loss?*

It's pretty much self-explanatory. It stops a loss. When you consider most private investors lose money, my argument to use them is made for me. Doing so stops all inevitable losses from getting too great. But let me give you the proper definition of a stop-loss: it's an order you set up at your trading platform which automatically sells a stock when its price reaches a set level (aka the stop price).

All decent and reputable brokers offer stop-loss functionality. If you place an order to buy shares in a company and that order is fulfilled you will be given the option to place a *sell* stop-loss on that stock. (Some will even let you set it at the time of buying.)

Example

This is how it works for me. Let's say I buy £1,000 of shares in a company. This stock then shows up within my portfolio on my account. I click *sell* and am presented with the option to sell all the shares I hold in that company or some of them. Let's just say I select, 'sell all'.

The next option I am presented with is the manner in which I want to sell. These are my options with my broker:

- quote and deal
- at best
- limit order
- stop-loss.

Quote and deal is only available during market opening hours (8 am to 4.30 pm) and means I ask for a live quote from the market. The brokers present me with a price and that price is available for 15 seconds. I can choose to accept it, reject it – or, if the 15 seconds expire, I can just refresh the quote.

At best is an order you give a broker to buy or sell shares at the best price available at the time the order is placed. You might need to use this if you can't get a quote (normally in small illiquid companies); perhaps you are trying to buy and there's heightened demand for the shares (due to positive news just being released) or you are trying to sell and there's increased supply (due to negative news just being released). You can also place these orders when the market is closed and it will get filled when the market opens.

Limit order lets you set a price for shares above which you won't buy and/or below which you won't sell. This can also be placed in conjunction with a stop-loss. This can also be placed outside market opening hours and will be executed, if the conditions are fulfilled, when the market opens.

And **stop-loss** allows you to set the price at which – if the share moves there – you want the broker to automatically sell. You can chose to sell some or all. A word of caution: stop-losses are not quite guaranteed. If stocks are in freefall, your level may get passed before your shares are sold. But that's rare. Some firms offer guaranteed stops (for a premium).

I only tend to use **quote and deal** and **stop-losses**.

Sometimes I will use **at best** as a last resort if I can't get a live quote and want to get into or out of a stock quickly.

How do I choose where to set stops?

Before I invest in a company, I look at the price and work out what the price is 20% lower, e.g. if I am buying a company priced at £1, I will automatically think, I need to insert a stop-loss at 80p.

Having said all this, 20% is not an iron rule. As you get more experienced, you can use charts to help set your stops with more sophistication (and this has particular benefits in microcaps, because their price movement can be so dramatic at times). I cover this in chapter 23. But a crude stop at 20% is better than no stop at all.

There are more than mechanical advantages to using stop-losses. Placing a stop-loss on my investments straightaway makes me think about the risk side of the investment. It automatically makes me work out how much I will lose *if* the investment goes wrong. That has all sorts of benefits.

When you buy a stock, you are hard wired as an investor to focus on the reward. After all, that is why you are investing – to make money. You have just done some research on the company and are convinced it will make you money and you are excited. You probably believe the stock price will take off and make you a stack of cash. You are likely to be the most emotionally attached to an investment when you make that initial investment.

When you are in this frame of mind you are not thinking about the investment going wrong. It couldn't be further from your mind. This is why most private investors go too big on their initial investment. They only think about the (big) reward.

The practice of thinking about and setting stop-losses brings risk to the forefront and helps you check your thinking. (As well as mechanically capping your losses.)

Nobody likes paying for insurance

When you buy a new car, you have to buy insurance for it. You do not buy a car with the intention of crashing it – but it could happen. When you are making your decision on the type of insurance policy you are going to buy, you run through a few of the worst-case scenarios to inform your decision.

Consider your stop-loss as your insurance policy. You do not intend the investment to go wrong but there are so many moving parts to an investment outside your control that *could* go wrong.

With an insurance policy, you don't enjoy paying for it but you are thankful for it when you have to use it. This is the same as a stop-loss. If you do your research correctly and place your stops at the right place, then more often than not *they will not be used* – but when they do get fulfilled you will be thankful.

There will be the odd time a stop will be triggered and the stock will rebound but for any time this happens there will be multiple times you will see a share price continue southwards after your stop kicks in.

I give an example later where a stock started dropping on high volume on no news. My stop kicked in and the share price kept going down. The next day the company released news on an investigation over a contract they had won.

Stop-losses can protect you against many leftfield, black swan events outside your control but also against your poor investment decisions (and there will be a few).

Face your fear

When you place stop-losses on all your investments you will know exactly how much you can lose if they all go wrong.

This might sound a bit depressing but it stops you overly focusing on the minute-by-minute movement of your holdings' prices. It also stops you wondering how big your loss on a stock will get before you make the decision to cut it (and in many instances you won't, as you may still be convinced it will get back to breakeven). "As soon as it gets back to breakeven I will sell" are the words of many a doomed investor.

Firstly, the further it falls the more unlikely it is to get back to breakeven. Secondly, if it does rise, you probably wouldn't sell as you'd start believing it's going to make you money again. Remember, shares do not go straight up or down. So a big losing stock, which is in a downtrend, will invariably bounce. This will give you some hope that all is not lost and the investment could become profitable. Then all of a sudden it reverts to a downtrend, making your loss bigger.

Stop-losses remove this uncertainty.

In short, using stop-losses is risk management. If you are not managing your risk, then you will not be able to manage your reward.

If you need another reason to cut your losses early then try this. The bigger your loss becomes, the harder it is to get back to breakeven. Look at the following table. It shows the gains you need to break even after a drop:

THIS IS THE GAIN YOU NEED TO BREAK EVEN AFTER A DROP	
% DROP	% RISE TO BREAK EVEN
10	11
15	18
20	25
25	33
30	43
35	54
40	67
45	82
50	100

Gains required after pains

If a share price drops 50%, you need a 100% gain to get back to breakeven. Any loss greater than 25% will become a struggle, as it needs a 33%+ gain to break even. This is an uphill struggle, just to not lose money. Sometimes you have to accept you got it wrong and move on.

If you need yet another reason to cut your losers, think about this. Imagine all the losses you have absorbed on all your biggest losers. Now cap all those losses at 20%. How much better would your portfolio look?

First and foremost, investing is about avoiding big losses. Then it's about making gains. These gains will be more pronounced if they are not dragged down by big losers. Big losers wipe out gains, so wipe out the big losers and you are left with the gains.

Stops and volume

If you find the size of your entire position is bigger than 10% of the average daily volume – which will only happen in small companies – you may find your stop-losses, if executed, could trigger the share price to drop. This in turn could then encourage other sellers and take out your next stop-loss.

So make sure the company you are investing into is liquid enough to absorb your sells without too much impact on the share price. It's also worth noting that average daily volume tends to increase on a stock that consistently rises. More on average daily volume later.

Stops and winners

The discipline of selling is important to get right too. And you can – and should – use stops for that. More on that in chapter 11.

8.
It's Your Money, Manage it Professionally

"I don't think it's productive to wallow in regret. But if you've lost money in a stock and you don't learn anything, that's wasted money. Figure out what it is that you did wrong and don't do it again."
—**Joel Tillinghast**

You are a fund manager

If you are investing in individual companies, you are a fund manager. This ties into portfolio management in a way. But it's a mindset shift as much as anything, so I want to deal with it separately.

OK, you may not receive a big juicy salary or get invited out to swanky business lunches in the City (or Wall Street) but you are *actively managing your funds*.

If you do not enjoy investing or researching companies then you are probably not going to do that well. As Mark Twain once said, "Find a job you enjoy doing, and you will never have to work a day in your life."

It may not be your job, but managing individual investments means you have to take an active role. This requires time.

If you don't have the time – or do not want to put the effort in – I would highly recommend sticking with a fund. Don't just make it the backbone. Make it the whole body of your investments. This means you become a passive investor.

After all, fund managers are paid to do this; it's their full-time job. And even then some people question whether they are that good at it. Remember the stat from earlier: nine out of ten actively managed funds failed to match the S&P 500 index performance over the previous 15 years. Hence why more and more private investors are deciding to invest in index funds.

Individual stock picking is not easy. Most active fund managers do not beat an index fund. So what makes you think you can?

The power of possibilities

I don't want to discourage you. I want to prepare you. If you enjoy investing, you *can* outperform fund managers. I have. There's also another advantage on the side of private investors. You can invest in microcaps on a smaller scale and be a lot nimbler.

OK, 90% of fund managers can't beat the S&P 500 index. That is like any other profession. The vast majority of people within any profession are not exceptional, by definition they can't be – but *you* can be an exceptional private investor.

I am often surprised when I see the types of companies some funds invest into and am therefore not surprised most of them can't beat the index. I have witnessed them investing into companies with no growth, or that lack value, or that are in a downtrend. You won't be doing that.

In the UK a lot of fund managers stick by the 5, 10, 40 rule. This means no one company should take up more than 10% of their fund and their top five holdings should not take up more than 40% of their fund.

So when a company starts outperforming and becomes 10% of their fund they have to cut it. You do not have to do this. As long as you protect your downside, you can really let your winners run. If you are lucky to pick a ten-bagger (1,000% return) how gutted would you be if you cut it after it's gone up 100%?

You can also cut your losers quicker at a certain level without any liquidity problems. I have often seen funds hold on to losing investments way too long. You shouldn't. If a stock starts losing you should limit your downside – while not limiting your upside on exceptional winners.

There's yet another reason you should beat fund managers. Because it's your money. So you should care more. Remember this: if you are managing your own money you are your own fund manager.

A side note: be wary of financial advisors. They will charge you a fee to buy a mix of active and passive funds. You can invest into those yourself without incurring their fee.

So the question is: can you beat the majority of fund managers who are paid handsomely to do it full time? The answer is yes. If you put the effort in and have the discipline to stick to some of the principles in this book, you can *significantly* outperform them.

9.
The Backbone

"You can only know so many companies. If you're managing 50 or 100 positions, the chances that you can add value are much, much lower."
—**Lou Simpson**

The best of both worlds

I predominantly invest in small companies, which can be very volatile. In short, they rise at a faster rate than big companies, especially in a bull market, but also do the opposite in a bear market. My hope is I pick a small company that can grow into a medium-sized company.

However, if I only invest in small companies then I am going to suffer an outsized fall during a bear market (and have). It's putting all my eggs in one basket.

In 2018, towards the end of the last bull market, I started putting a regular amount of money into Vanguard's **LifeStrategy 100% Equity Fund**. This fund has broad exposure to shares of UK companies and non-UK companies, including emerging markets. It holds roughly 7,000 different companies, 40% UK, 60% rest of the world.

This was the correct thing to do – as discussed in chapter 7, a portfolio needs a backbone. However, towards the end of any bull market, stocks start to rally really strongly. This often happens as the stock market doing well tends to be talked about, even making mainstream news. Friends who have already invested tell their friends (who don't normally invest) how well they are doing and they start piling in too, pushing prices even higher. This is why most new investors tend to invest at the top of the market. Nobody talks about the market at the bottom, because most private investors are sitting on losses. They are less inclined to share this information than when they are sitting on gains.

In 2020, I became greedy and decided I could make more out of individual stocks. So I withdrew my fund money and put it into individual stocks. Initially I did well in these investments – but, as said, microcaps are more volatile.

My portfolio dropped by around 45%. If I'd kept, say, a third of my money in the Vanguard LifeStrategy Fund, my portfolio would have fared better – it dropped by less than 10% during this period.

Microcaps are powerful. But you need to diversify.

You could put a percentage of your money into fixed income investments like government bonds, which are safe and pay you a return based on current interest rates. As I write this, interest rates are 5.25% and you can get a 6% yield on government bonds. However, I prefer and know more about equities – and rates of interest will not stay at this level for long.

So what I've chosen to do is put 1% of my total portfolio value, on a monthly basis, into a low-cost high-yielding dividend-paying fund. The provider is BlackRock and the epic code is **IUKD**. Its total expense ratio (the fee they charge) is 0.4%. I use my current cash holding to fund this. If this cash runs low, I pause this recurring investment until a stop-loss on an individual stock kicks in, freeing up funds to carry on.

This fund invests in the highest-dividend-yielding 50 companies in the FTSE 350 (the biggest 350 companies listed in the UK). I am not recommending this fund; there are plenty of other funds out there. I choose this fund because it pays a nice dividend that is currently re-invested. This provides a compound growth effect. For example, if I have £100,000 invested in this fund and they pay me 5% in dividends, I will receive £5,000 for the first year. Rather than take these dividends, I reinvest them back into the fund. This means in year two I will not only be paid 5% on my initial £100,000 but on the £5,000 I was paid and reinvested last year. Five per cent of £105,000 is £5,250, which is a 5% increase on last year's payment. So I am being paid dividends on my dividends. Over the long term this has a powerful compounding effect.

Example

If you'd invested in the FTSE 100 index over the last 20 years, not taking any dividend income into account, the value would have increased by just over 40%. However, the total return including reinvested dividends is 193% over the same period. Almost five times the return of the raw index.

As I write this, the FTSE 100 has just hit a new all-time high of 8313 but has still majorly underperformed US indices. Even at this all-time high the FTSE 100 is still relatively cheap. The price-to-earnings (P/E) ratio of the FTSE 100 is around 10 times, whereas for the S&P 500 it's around 20. In other words, you pay twice as much for the earnings of those US firms as you do for the UK firms. The FTSE 100 also has a current dividend yield of around 4% whereas the S&P 500 pays a lower yield of less than 1.5.%.

In the future I may take these dividends as income but for now I want to build it up to the point where the income would, if I needed it, provide me with a decent yearly wage.

What type of diversification is it?

You might think: *You invest in UK companies but also invest in a UK-based fund. Surely this isn't diversifying?*

You're partly correct. However, FTSE 100 companies are largely international businesses that generate most of their revenues abroad. So they are very different businesses to the smaller companies that are constituents of AIM. As a comparison, the AIM All-Share – which is where the majority of my individual investments in microcaps sit – is valued, in its entirety, on a market capitalisation basis at approximately £100 billion. The largest company in my fund, HSBC, is valued at £130 billion. It also derives most of its revenue from the Far East.

Whichever fund you pick, make sure it's low cost and well diversified. Vanguard funds are generally good value. Some of my friends are invested in the Vanguard LifeStrategy 100 Fund, which holds over 6,000 companies, including many of the biggest companies in the US, UK and Europe. Its ongoing charge is 0.22%.

The closer you get to your retirement, the less exposed you should be to riskier individual investments. Vanguard also has products for this called Target Retirement funds. Depending on your age, these funds automatically adjust your exposure to shares and bonds. The older you get, the more bonds (because less volatile, in theory).

You pick the Target Retirement Fund closest to your planned retirement date or within five years after that, then you just let it run. So if you intend to retire in 2040, you pick their **Target Retirement Fund 2040**, which would currently have a 25% exposure to bonds and a 75% exposure to shares (as shares are generally higher risk/reward to bonds).

Every five years these funds rebalance, reducing exposure to shares by 5% and increasing the exposure to bonds by 5%.

The other LifeStrategy funds also diversify between bonds and stocks – e.g. LifeStrategy 80 is 80% in stocks, LifeStrategy 60 is 60% in stocks, and so on.

No investment strategy is 100% bulletproof; if you want reward, you need to take risk. There has always been a generally accepted rule that passive investors should have a split between shares and bonds of 60/40. Bonds are supposed to be safe and they generally are, but their prices have collapsed in the last two years, blowing a hole in this 60/40 strategy.

I would prefer a well-diversified all-equity fund. This will ensure you get exposure to some of the best businesses in the world. I understand what moves the share prices of businesses more than I understand what moves the bond market.

For my sons I put a regular amount into **Vanguard's S&P 500 fund**, which tracks the US index that holds the 500 biggest companies in America. The ongoing charge there is just 0.07%.

Always look at the fees involved. They can seriously impact your returns over the long term (and that is how long you should hold a fund). If a fund charges you, say, 2%, given the long-term return of the S&P is ~10%, they are not taking 2% of your money – but 20% of your returns. I do not think that any of Vanguard's funds charge over 0.5%. As I said, there are hundreds if not thousands of funds out there to choose from – however, BlackRock and Vanguard are the two biggest providers.

Eggs and chickens

So back to my portfolio. Holding a fund means I not only contain eggs with unhatched chicks but fully grown chickens too.

I invest in eggs (microcaps) with the hope they hatch and grow into chickens. However, by investing in this big fund, which holds mature companies, I am also getting the benefits of owning chickens too.

In summary, here are three reasons you should hold a fund – even while investing in individual shares:

1. Stability

It reduces portfolio volatility. Holding many big companies will always be less volatile than a few small companies.

2. Diversity

Holding a fund means you achieve instant low-cost diversification. If you had to buy the amount of companies included in a fund individually, your cost in acquisition fees would not be economically viable.

3. Probability

You will have a higher chance of a positive return. Monthly investment into a low-cost, well-diversified fund will give you a higher probability of a positive return than picking individual companies.

A low-cost, well-diversified fund should be your retirement safety net. If your individual investments don't pay off, you will still have a decent-sized nest egg.

How much should you allocate to a fund?

The percentage of your portfolio a fund will ultimately take up should depend on your age and experience. A fund should take up more of your portfolio the closer you are to retirement.

However, the system I have created below will ensure your allocation to your fund will reflect your performance on your individual investments. This means if you don't do so well in these individual investments, you still have your fund to fall back on.

If these individual investments play out, then they just become a bigger part of your portfolio, the profits from which can be used to pay into the safer liquid fund.

Example 1 – A beginning active investor

Let's say you have £100,000, and you put £75,000 into a fund, and in a year it generates a 5% return. It would be worth £78,750. You might do this if you're just starting out and getting used to investing.

If you manage to make 30% on your £25,000 individual investments they would be worth £32,500. Together your portfolio would be worth £111,250.

These individual investments now take up 29% of your portfolio value and your fund takes up 71%. So already you are taking more risk as your individual companies have become a larger part of your portfolio. (It's worth noting that, during a bull market, you may be able to generate 30% from individual investments but this is not likely achievable in a correction or a bear market.)

If your individual companies don't perform as well and their value drops by 20%, they would be worth £20,000.

Your fund is more likely to return a consistent 5%+ as it's more diversified into mature companies. So let's say it does 5%. Even with this drop in your individual investments your total portfolio value would still be worth £98,750. So you've only lost 1.25%.

If you continue with this strategy over the next 20 years, making 5% on your fund and losing 20% per annum on your individual stocks, you would still make money in year four and double your money by year 20, just with the gains on the fund.

This is the worst-case scenario as you'd have to be a very bad stock picker to manage to lose 20% a year every single year in a 20-year run. Also this 20% per annum loss wouldn't happen if you take quick losses, rather than hold on to big ones, as I described earlier and will show later.

As I write this I currently have around 29% in my fund but keep allocating 1% of my total portfolio value to this fund on a monthly basis.

You may be thinking,

Hang on, in 71 months, the fund will take up 100% of your portfolio won't it?

If my fund's performance beats my individual stocks then over time it will take up more of my portfolio. However, if my individual stocks outperform my fund (which is the goal) then they will take up more of a share.

Example 2 – A struggling active investor

Let's say right now I have 100% of £100,000 invested in individual stocks. So I choose to take 1% or £1,000 per month out of my individual investments and put it into my fund. This might be the approach of an investor struggling with returns from active investing and now adopting the system set out here.

At the end of year one, if my individual investments make no money but my fund generates 5%, my fund would be worth £12,600 and my individual investments would be worth £88,000. As my total portfolio value is now worth £100,600, my fund takes up 12.5% of my portfolio and my individual investments account for 87.5%.

If I maintain this performance (generating no return on my individual investments but putting £1,000 a month from them into my fund and achieving a 5% return on this) by the end of year two my fund will already be taking up 25% of my total portfolio value.

So due to the underperformance on my individual investments I am already automatically diversifying away from them.

If this underperformance in my individual investments persists by year eight, my portfolio value will be worth £124,319, with my fund taking up 97% of it and my individual investments only accounting for 3%.

Example 3 – A thriving active investor

On a simplified basis, if you have a portfolio value of £100,000 and are allocating £12,000 (12%) a year to your fund, you need to achieve a return greater than 12% from your individual investments to prevent your fund from dominating your portfolio.

Let's say you have a portfolio value worth £100,000 and you decide to allocate 5% a year to your fund. You achieve a return of 10% on your individual investments, and 5% on your fund. Your allocation to your fund comes from your individual investments.

If you start off on year one with £95,000 invested in individual stocks and £5,000 into a fund, by year eight your portfolio would be worth £194,000; 75.3% of that would still be in individual investments and 24.7% would be allocated to a fund.

If you are very confident in generating a positive return on your individual investments then maybe you should consider allocating less of a percentage of your total portfolio value to your fund.

But be careful not to get too greedy, like I did at the end of the last bull market. Do not be tempted to raid your fund in order to overexpose on individual investments. A fund will stabilise the volatility of your portfolio, which you'll be thankful for in a correction or a bear market.

In essence, then, the system does require some individual discernment when setting the initial balance. But the 1% rule – of adding 1% of the total portfolio value passively every month – will naturally steer you to safety. If you're new, 75% in passive and 25% in active is reasonable in my opinion. I always try to keep a cash reserve to fund this investment. Remember risk and reward.

Beat your fund

The point of owning individual companies is to achieve a better return than you would get from a fund, otherwise you might as well just hold a fund. However, with the potential of greater rewards from exposure to individual companies, comes a greater risk. So keep an eye on this.

If you underperform on your individual investments but continue to allocate a regular amount to your fund, and this outperforms, you will automatically be diversifying towards your better-performing investments.

Pound (dollar) cost averaging

Regardless of which percentage level you choose to allocate to a fund, I would suggest you do not put this entire amount into a fund in one go. There is evidence that lump-sum investing (putting all your cash into an investment in one go) outperforms dollar or pound-cost averaging (where you drip it in over time, averaging out the buy price through ups and downs). However, I would suggest that it depends on what investment you pick and when you choose to invest. You could happen to pick a market top. No doubt it will recover and do well over time – but it will be a painful wait while it does. This pain may also get so emotionally overpowering that you could pull your investment close to a market bottom. Buying low and selling high isn't as easy as it sounds, and you'd be surprised by how many private investors do the exact opposite due to general market sentiment. Everyone is bullish at the top and bearish at the bottom. So try to spread your allocation over 12–36 months. That way you will automatically buy plenty of dips and corrections, plus benefit from a rising market.

I allocate 1% of my total portfolio value to my fund on a monthly basis. This means I am dollar (pound) cost averaging. Investing set amounts at regular intervals over a long period of time can help you manage timing risk. This is because you do not have to try to guess where the best price is to buy or worry if you're buying at the top or bottom of the market, because you are buying regularly.

Let's say you invest £100 every month. When the market is up, your £100 will buy fewer shares in this fund, but when the market is down, your money will buy more shares in this fund.

Over time, this strategy could lower your average cost per share compared to what you would have paid if you'd bought all your shares at once. Do not be tempted to put all your allocation into a fund in one go. You could be buying at the top of the market or at a time when the market is about to undergo a correction. It will take you a long time to recover these paper losses and reduce your potential retirement pot.

Most stockbrokers provide you with the option of setting up a regular investment plan. As I said before, I selected the monthly option. If you have less exposure to a fund your performance on individual investments has to be a lot better.

10.
Is Investing Gambling?

"Fortunes are made and lost by thousands of men in the stock market; they are made and kept by a few dozen."
—**Edwin Lefèvre**

Limit your losses, maximise your gains

The overall strategy of this book is to limit losses in addition to a robust stock-picking strategy which means you maximise gains on your winners. Hopefully this shouldn't be too much of a stretch.

If you follow this strategy correctly, your portfolio will hold and leverage towards winners, while limiting your losers. The question is: *How do you find winners?*

I will cover this in the following chapters but as I have pointed out already, it's very important that you structure your portfolio correctly so you do not go overweight on your losers and underweight on your winners.

In short, to ensure your investments provide you with an overall positive return your portfolio needs to be geared towards your winners and not your losers. Private investors tend to do the opposite, which is often described as watering your weeds and cutting your flowers.

How do you know which companies will turn out to be winners and which will be losers?

You don't. Not until they start winning or losing.

Sometimes you can do all the research you want and believe a stock is a no brainer but it will still underperform. Or a company you weren't quite convinced about can really take off. The solution is to give all stocks an equal chance. By this I mean applying relatively equal exposure initially. Then only increasing exposure when the winners start to reveal themselves.

Horses for courses

Here's a horsey analogy.

When would it be easier to spot the winning horse in a race? Just after the race has started? Or after the majority of the race has been run?

With that in mind, let's say you are going to bet on the Grand National. Many will say investing and gambling are not the same, and in certain respects that's true – but gambling is defined by the *Encyclopaedia Brittanica* as "The betting or staking of something of value, with consciousness of risk and hope of gain".

And that's a pretty good definition of investing.

They're also similar in that both are games of probability. As are most things in life.

Back to the Grand National. You obviously want to win but there are 30 horses taking part in the race. How do you pick a winner?

If you look at previous races, over the last 20 years, the average odds of the winning horse are 24 to 1.

Obviously this means sometimes a horse will come in at shorter odds, sometimes at greater odds. But this means you could back 20 out of the 30 horses, with an equal stake – let's say £1 – and if the average odds theme plays out, and you win, you would walk away with £4 profit or 20% (24 × £1 = £24 - £20 = £4).

Backing two thirds of the field gives you a higher chance of backing the winner than if you just backed one horse. You have a 66% chance of picking a winner rather than a 3.33% chance if you only bet on one horse.

Now let's say the betting rules of the race allow you to change your bets up to the point where 75% of the race is complete – but you can only use the money already staked.

You are watching the race and with only 25% of the race left you notice ten of your horses are in the leading pack. So you figure there's a high probability of one of these horses winning. You move your stakes from the ten horses you've backed that do not look to be in contention, on to the ten leading horses. You now have a £2 bet on each of these ten horses with a better chance of winning. If the average odds game plays out, this would mean you collect £48 for a win.

That's a profit of £28 or 140% (24 × £2 = £48 - £20 = £28). A lot better than if you'd stuck with your losers.

Calculating your exposure

With investing you can not only do exactly what I have just described, but you can add extra cash to your winning investments. Now, in the scenario just given would you ever consider taking money off your winners and adding it to the horses that looked like they were never going to win?

A lot of private investors do this, including me. I have averaged down (or doubled down) on my underperforming shares.

NEVER DO THIS!!! BACK THE WINNERS, NOT THE LOSERS!!!

Having stated this, there is an exception. If you make an investment and start small but the share price goes down, you can choose to do something or nothing. You can choose to add a stop-loss and take a small loss. Or, if you believe the original investment thesis is intact, then you can do nothing.

Sometimes even if the business is a good one, i.e. it has good growth and is of good value, if momentum is not present the share price can drop (I cover this later).

If you do nothing because you still believe the company has potential and you've started small, it will not impact your portfolio value too much.

You could wait until the share price gains momentum and starts an uptrend, then buy more. Depending how far the price has fallen since you initially bought it, this new uptrend could start below your initial buy price. So you are technically averaging down – but it's now in an uptrend, and if the company's fundamentals are still sound, you are investing in a company at a better valuation and so it has more potential.

A word of warning, though: if you buy a company whose share price is in a downtrend, the time it takes for the trend to end and revert to an uptrend can be measured in months. (And that's the best-case scenario. Worse-case scenario, it could be a year – or never.) So sometimes it pays to cut early and move your money on to the next potential winner or look to find another winner.

In the following examples, when I refer to exposure I mean the percentage of your total portfolio value. I use the example of a £100,000 portfolio but I am fully aware most people do not have a portfolio this size. I only use £100,000 as it's easy to show examples in regards to percentages. So if your initial investment is between 1 and 3%, this is £1,000 to £3,000.

However, if your portfolio value is £10,000 then between 1 and 3% is only £100 to £300, which means dealing costs take up a greater percentage of your costs. So you may need to adjust these percentages.

In any case, before you invest think: how much can I *lose* on this investment? This should provide you with an initial level of investment you will feel comfortable with. Whatever you do, do not think: how much can I *make* on this investment?

My initial exposure level can vary from 1% to 3%. The level depends on the company I am investing into. If my portfolio value is £100,000 my initial investment will be between £1,000 and £3,000.

Why this amount? And how do I decide between where on the scale to go?

It depends on the company and its liquidity.

If I regard the company as a higher risk/reward investment (maybe a **recovery play** – more on this later) I will invest just 1% of my total portfolio value. If it's a growing, profitable, undervalued company, in an uptrend (a **performer** – more on this later) I could invest 3% of my total portfolio value. It's less risky, so I can risk more.

In both cases my exposure is also dictated by the liquidity of a company's shares. If I invest £10,000 in a company and this value is above the average daily volume of a company (the amount of shares that change hands on a typical day), I could run into issues getting live quotes. I will cover this in more detail later but it always pays to check out the average daily volume of a company's shares as it affects the spread (the difference between the bid – or sell – price, and the ask – or buy – price) and whether you can get into and out of a company in a position size you require.

My initial investment of 1 to 3% means it's not enough to get in trouble but it's enough to care. This is not to say I will lose the entire 1% or 3% – I will put in a stop-loss to take me out if it drops 20% below my buy price.

I'm only actually risking between 0.2% to 0.6% of my total portfolio value (20% of 1% or 3% of my total portfolio value).

Remember, losses are painful – but they become more painful the bigger they get. **Keep your losses small.**

You can do the opposite with your winners and make them bigger. I'll go into that in a moment in chapter 11.

Dealing with losers

Do not be tempted to average down on a loser, because this will leverage your portfolio towards your losers. It is reinforcing failure in the hope of a pleasant surprise. I can't say this enough: letting losses grow is the number one mistake private investors make, and it can impact your portfolio massively.

Example

For simplicity, let's say my portfolio value is a nice round £100,000 and I risk £3,000 on my initial investment. Using a 20% stop-loss means I will sell the company when I'm down £600. Simple, done, out.

Starting with a small exposure will help you perform better for three reasons:

1. Less painful

You will be more likely to cut a loser quickly as the pain won't be as great if it were a bigger holding.

2. Portfolio effect

Losers cannot become too big, meaning they won't drag down your overall portfolio value.

3. Efficient allocation of capital

You will only consider increasing your exposure to companies performing, meaning your portfolio will be more leveraged to your winners.

In summary, keep your losses small and your winners big.

11.
How Many and How Much?

"I think the secret is if you have a lot of stocks, some will do mediocre, some will do OK, and if one or two of 'em go up big time, you produce a fabulous result."
—Peter Lynch

How many stocks should you hold?

I've had discussions with many investors on the question of how many stocks you should hold – and they've all been wrong. Or they consider me to be wrong. In other words, it's very subjective.

It's like trying to argue about who is a better band, The Beatles or The Rolling Stones. I think it's The Beatles but if you prefer The Rolling Stones I'm never going to convince you.

There is no definitive answer so I will give you my opinion, having tried holding many shares and a few shares. If you hold a low-cost, well-diversified fund, as I do, then you're already diversified. It's important to remember that.

My fund holds 50 mature dividend-paying companies. So there is no point in acquiring a load of other big mature companies that pay dividends; it defeats the object of holding a fund and is an inefficient way of diversifying.

This could be described as **diworsification**.

Meaning, lowering the quality of your portfolio by adding lower-quality investment ideas.

The more stocks you hold, generally, the less risk there is to your portfolio value. This is because holding many stocks means they take up less of a percentage of your total portfolio value. If one bombs it does not really negatively impact your portfolio value.

If a stock only takes up 1% of your total portfolio value and the business goes bust you have only lost 1%. However, this cuts both ways. Holding small positions also means the reward won't be as big if one becomes a winner. And having too many companies is hard to keep track of.

I personally find it hard to manage more than **20 companies**. This is the job of a fund manager and they do not do research on their own, they have researchers to help them.

You are investing in businesses. Every one is unique, with different management, products, services and financial metrics. There's a lot of information to absorb on each one. Holding 50 companies you know little about is more of a risk than having ten companies you know a lot about.

Stocks you hold should be akin to the children you have. If you can't name them without some help, you probably have too many.

If you are considering making a new investment, ideally it should be a better investment than the last one you made. If it isn't, it may drag the performance of your portfolio down. If you're not confident it can generate better returns than your last investment then you shouldn't invest in it. You should do more research. Adding stocks to your portfolio should add value, not subtract it.

This is why I like to stick to a maximum number of stocks. This ensures quality over quantity.

Let's look at extremes. Say my portfolio is worth £100,000 and I invest £1,000 into a company.

Looking at risk first, if its share price drops by 50% then I have only lost £500 (out of £100,000) or 0.5% (unless I use a stop-loss). That's not too bad. However, if the share price rises by 50%, a decent rise, I will only make £500 or 0.5%.

A 50% rise is a very good gain. I feel like I should benefit more from such a winner.

So the question is, *how do I keep my risk small but maximise my reward?* If my initial exposure on any stock is 1 to 3% (of my total portfolio value) and I keep it at this level, even a ten-bagger is not going to have a big positive impact on my portfolio value.

If my portfolio is valued at £100,000 and I invest 1% into a stock (£1,000) and it becomes a ten-bagger, it would be worth £10,000. OK, it's a great return on that particular investment – but ten-baggers are rare, and if I manage to find one I want a decent return overall, and for that to be reflected in my portfolio value.

As I mentioned previously, you need to back your winners, because these are good businesses doing something right and this tends to endure. So if a company rises, you should look at increasing your exposure to it. Let's look at the best approach to that.

The seeds of success

When you initially invest in companies, you can't guarantee which will do well and which will not. And you can't say for certain which companies will provide you with a decent return and which will give you outstanding returns, as businesses are always evolving. The directors of one business you're invested in may make a decision that is not going to play out well, the directors of another business could choose to make an operational shift that will be a game changer.

So all these initial positions you make in companies are just **seed investments**. Like seeds you plant, you cannot guarantee which will sprout first, nor do you know which will grow the most.

If you have planted five seeds in five different pots and three sprout at roughly the same time but one seems to be growing the fastest, do you ignore this and water the two pots that are not growing?

If you do this, it's tantamount to doubling down on your losers. What you would do is water the three thriving plants, especially the biggest one, because it needs more water.

This is how you should look at your portfolio. Do not invest any more money into any company until it's quite obvious you have a winner on your hands. Like the biggest plant among two others, a stock growing faster than its peers stands out and will attract attention. Then other people will also be watering it (or investing money into it), which provides **momentum**. Buyers are attracted to rising prices, which fuels momentum further.

I will explain how I attempt to average up later.

Maximum exposure?

How much should my maximum exposure on one stock be?

There is no hard and fast rule to this but this next sentence is going to seem strange, especially when I keep advising you to beware of risk.

As long as a company's share price keeps going up, you should keep buying it – but there are three caveats to this:

Caveat one

This is as long as the company keeps releasing excellent financial results showing they are still growing at a good rate (around 20% topline) and they are not overvalued. If that's the case, then there's still potential. So be careful of buying before results. You are better off waiting for a trading update or financial results (full year or interims) to confirm they are still growing and of good value.

If their share price rises after these results, don't fret about having missed out – it's confirmation you are invested in a good company. I have been guilty of trying to get ahead of results by buying beforehand. This invariably does not play out well for two reasons.

1. Companies' share prices often rise toward results, then dip on their release.
2. There could be something negative in the results that was not revealed in the trading update.

In any case, waiting for results gives you more information on a company.

Caveat two

I do not feel comfortable putting more than 10% of my total portfolio value into an individual company. As mentioned, I prefer 1 to 3%. But this is not the same as having a company take up more than 10% of my portfolio due to its share price rising.

For example, if my portfolio value is £100,000 and I invest 3% (£3,000) of my total portfolio value into a company, then it rises by 400%, it would now be worth £12,000 (if all of my other investments largely remained the same). This means it would now be taking up 10.7% of my total portfolio value. As long as I have a stop-loss to lock in this profit then I am comfortable with this; it proves I have invested in a good company doing well. It could continue to do well so I do not want to limit this upside. I have only risked 3% of my portfolio value.

This is different from putting 15% of my total portfolio value into an investment. If I did this I would be risking £15,000 of my own money. If this started going wrong, I would find it emotionally harder to cut.

Caveat three

If you are investing in a microcap, you should always pay attention to the average daily volume of that company. I mentioned this briefly earlier. It is the amount of shares traded over a period (normally 30 days) then divided by 30 to give you the average daily volume.

This shows you how liquid – how regularly traded and available – a company's stock is.

These metrics are published on most websites like TradingView or Investing.com, including my website where the average daily volume is also converted in pounds. Any daily volume worth less than £100,000 is highlighted in red. The reason for this is because you do not want to find yourself stuck in a stock, especially if you want to get out, due to lack of liquidity.

As a rule of thumb, if the average daily volume is worth around £100,000 then on a normal day – if the company has released no news – around 50% of the transactions will be people buying and 50% will be investors selling.

If the company releases positive news, that volume will increase – with a bigger percentage of investors buying than selling. So a good day to sell would be on a positive news day because there's plenty of demand for your shares. But we all know most people do not sell on a positive news day when the share price is rising, and you should not limit your upside.

If a company releases bad news then the percentage of shares being sold, in relation to the daily volume, increases. The actual volume will also be above the average daily volume, so there's more liquidity – but, nevertheless, depending on how bad the news is, selling could make up between 60 to 90% of the volume. Therefore you have a smaller number of buyers wanting to take the stock off a larger number of sellers. Essentially most people are rushing for the exit at the same time, but the exit isn't big enough for everyone to fit through.

You do not want to be unable to sell if you want to sell. To be on the safe side, be careful if you are holding more than 10% of the average daily volume of a company. For example, if the average daily volume is £100,000 and you are holding a lot more than £10,000 in stock, you may have an issue selling if negative news lands.

When I say you won't be able to sell, this is not strictly true. You may not be able to get a live quote to sell. There are a few different options when it comes to buying and selling, as we saw earlier. If you are trying to sell on a day the company releases negative news, the market makers (a firm or individual who actively quotes two-sided markets in a particular stock by providing bids and offers along with the market size of each) are inundated with sell orders. Therefore they will be having issues matching sellers to buyers. To facilitate this they drop the price and widen the spread (the difference between the buy (offer) and sell (bid) prices quoted for a stock) to incentivise buyers, but also ensure they themselves have a level of safety, as this is how they earn money.

In this case you may only be able to sell with the **at best** option, which is the best price the market maker will get for you. When it comes to selling, accepting an at best order is the worst option – as you never know what price you will get.

The amount of a stock you hold will not be an issue in bigger companies but it can be in microcaps – so just be aware of this.

Limit your downside, never limit your upside

I mentioned earlier why I like microcaps: if it's a good company, it can end up worth many times its current value. You need to take advantage of this.

Which brings me back to stops. You should never sell a company just because it's winning, never take a profit early. It's imperative you **let your winners run**.

Not doing so is the other big mistake private investors make.

Usually investors who keep losing money are not used to being in profit so they are desperate not to lose that little gain – and they take it too early. This is why you should use stop-losses set at certain levels, not just randomly sell a winner without knowing where it could go to.

The biggest amount of downside on any investment is 100% (or less if you use a stop-loss).

What's the biggest amount of upside on any investment?

Sky's the limit!

So it makes sense to limit your downside but *never* limit your upside. Which means: don't set stop-losses as a kind of price target. Keep them below the current price. Give that thing room to grow!

If you manage to find a company that goes on to be a **superstock** – by this I mean it rises by 1,000% or more – if you play it correctly you only need one big winner in your lifetime. However, you have to play it correctly – because these superstocks are rare. Never miss the chance to make lots of money from them.

If sitting on a big loser is the worst emotional experience in investing then what comes a close second is selling a stock and seeing it take off to the moon without you on board. All you need is an outstanding performer to transform your portfolio, if you are diversified properly and leverage your winners.

Example

Say my portfolio is worth £100,000 and I invest 3% of my total portfolio value into a company and put a stop-loss 20% below my initial buy-in price to make sure any loser doesn't get too big. My first goal is for the share price to rise by 20%. If this happens, I can move my stop-loss up to my initial buy-in price.

This means I have achieved the ultimate goal I can *ever achieve* in any investment: **a risk-free investment!**

This is the promised land of investments. Investing is all about risk vs reward. Once you get to put a stop-loss in that removes the risk side of the equation, all you are left with is... **reward** or breakeven (a breakeven is rare).

The most important thing is, you **can't lose money**. Think about that. You can't lose money.

Remember, most private investors do not make money because they hold on to their losers too long. These losses become bigger and bigger, they even double down, further leveraging their portfolio to their losers. When you achieve a risk-free stage in an investment, you can't lose.

This automatically removes the biggest mistake most private investors make.

All you need to do now is not sell your winner too early. This is one of the reasons I love investing: it gives you the ability to enjoy a risk-free investment.

This may not sound like a big deal but there are very few opportunities like this in the business world. Try to think of any other business investment where this could happen. They don't really exist. Products can fail, customers can leave, leads can dry up. There are no guarantees.

With investing, as long as you get to the point where you are 20% or more up, you should never lose money on that investment if you insert a stop-loss above your buy price (I suggest 20% below the current price).

In the past I have been in profit by over 200% in a company and ended up losing money, simply because I had not used stop-losses to lock in my profit.

Never make this mistake!

So to answer the question I asked many pages ago...

How many stocks should I have?

The more stocks you have, within a limit, the more likely you are to find some winners – but you're also more likely to find some losers too. It's not about quantity but quality.

You also do not want to use all your money buying lots of stocks. If you have 30 stocks taking up 3% of your total portfolio value, you have no cash to increase exposure to your winners.

As I mentioned, this is not about diversifying, because if you hold a fund, you've already done this. This is about finding winners and avoiding losers. It's about finding companies that can outperform the returns you get from your fund.

So as a general rule of thumb I would say that around 10–20 companies give you plenty of options to capture a good winner. This is if you've applied the principles in the following chapters.

If you hold ten stocks, all taking up 1 to 3% of your portfolio, it means you have 70 to 90% left to average up when your winners start to show themselves. But don't forget about your fund. The percentage this fund takes up determines the amount of companies you hold. Because you need available funds to average up on winners.

So if your fund takes up 75% of your total portfolio value you only have 25% left to invest. I would personally invest in 10 companies, allocating 1% of your total portfolio to each.

This means you have 15% left to allocate to winners when they start winning. You might think ten companies isn't a lot – but remember, this isn't about diversifying. You are already diversified with your fund. That's one of the great benefits.

This is about finding winners – and, if they do win, allocating more capital to them. They will then take up a greater percentage of your portfolio, which means you will have more exposure to winners than losers.

Let's say you allocate 50% to a fund and have 50% to allocate to individual companies. I would suggest investing in 15 companies, each taking up 1 to 3% of your portfolio, meaning you have 20 to 35% on the sidelines to allocate towards winners.

If you adopt a higher-risk strategy – i.e. you allocate 25% or less to a low-cost, well-diversified fund – you would have 75% of your portfolio in individual stocks. That means more companies, and probably starting at least 3%. Not for beginners. You need experience in research and handling your emotions. And you'll have to spend much more of your time on investing. It's not for everyone. But now you know how many and how much.

12.
Winners Keep on Winning, Losers Keep on Losing

"Some stocks go up 20–30% and they get rid of it and hold onto the dogs. And it's sort of like watering the weeds and cutting out the flowers. You want to let the winners run."
—**Peter Lynch**

Back your winners

During the bull market I used to average down – buy more of shares when they fell – and was convinced this was *the* strategy to make big money. And it did work for me from time to time. However, it can really go wrong, especially during a correction, a bear market or if a company's operations are underperforming. Averaging down can result in fatal losses. In short, it is not an effective risk management strategy.

Imagine you are a surfer. You are in the sea, sitting on your board facing out to sea, watching the waves at a distance, trying to read which will be the one that will take you in to the beach. You spot one that seems to be the right shape and the right height, so you position yourself to ride it.

As it gets closer, it doesn't build. It doesn't get to the size you require.

Do you go with it anyway? If you do, you know it will be a waste of time and you could miss a better wave.

Experienced surfers know which waves have the highest probability of giving them a good ride. Sometimes they will pick the wrong wave that won't live up to expectations but they will not pretend it's good and try to style it out by riding it in to the beach.

They will not disagree with the sea.

They bail out early and paddle back to find a new wave. Trying to ride a dud wave is the equivalent to averaging down on losers when it comes to investing. If an investment starts losing, don't chase it and double down. **You should not fight the market: it will always win.**

Sometimes surfers may pick a wave they think shows some promise, even though they are not truly convinced of its potential. They go with it anyway – and it turns out to be a great wave. This is the same with investing. You can do as much research as possible but you do not really know how well it's going to work out. If it does work out, go with it, make the best of it. Yes, you have to be selective – but if you do not try to ride the wave that looks promising, you will never find out.

However, you should not try to ride every wave you see. There has to be a level of quality control – just not so rigid that you miss out on a surprise winner.

I have made the mistake of not investing in a company that I thought was a little overvalued, even while growth and momentum was present. And I have got out of a company just because the share price did not rise and I got bored with it. Never limit the upside – only the downside.

Examples

Two really gutting examples are those of **AudioBoom (BOOM)** and **Argo Blockchain (ARB)**. Audioboom hosts podcasts and I was well aware of its rise in popularity as I host my own. I also interviewed the CEO quite a few times, who was a great salesman. I invested in Audioboom in 2019 at around 150p a share. The shares went nowhere for over 12 months. I eventually got bored and sold mid-2020 at a small loss. In January 2021 the share price broke out of this trading range and by February 2022 the share price hit 2250p. That was a 1,400% rise I missed out on.

I invested into Argo Blockchain in July of 2020 at around 5p. It is a Bitcoin miner and interest in Bitcoin was picking up. The price of Bitcoin was also starting to rise, so I figured this rise would be reflected in Argo's share price. It wasn't. The price oscillated between 5p and 10p for over a year. I sold it at around the same price I bought it for. Then in November 2020 it broke the 10p level and by February 2021 it had hit 285p a share. That's a rise of 5,600%.

You have to put the research in – but you cannot know a company will work until it does. Let the market decide. All you have to do is find a wave with potential and stick with it if it starts working out. You also have to be prepared to bail when a wave is obviously not going to work.

Averaging up

In a bull market the general market is rising so, if you average down, you are essentially buying a dip. If you average down in a *bear* market, you are buying a downtrend, which can last for years and be very painful.

There's a famous saying, "Winners keep on winning, losers keep on losing". This is true to a certain extent. Momentum plays a big part in this observation.

There have been a lot of studies looking at the performance of companies hitting their **52-week highs vs 52-week lows**. (These are exactly what they sound like: a share's highest or lowest price in a year.) Even though companies hitting their 52-week high tend to outperform embattled counterparts, these studies miss the point. Trading companies experiencing either isn't a preferred method. It is too blunt. Companies hitting either could suffer **momentum exhaustion**. Momentum tends to take a long time to cease – but the breakdown in this force could be close to breaking at both a 52-week high or low.

Not every company hitting its 52-week high or lows carries on going in that direction. Some do, some don't. Just buying one that hits these milestones does not guarantee anything. If a company hits a 52-week high and keeps releasing positive news that suggests growth is ongoing, and if the valuation is still not stretched, it can keep performing. If it's overvalued and news being released can't justify this valuation, the price will struggle to continue its rise.

If a company hits a 52-week low and releases news that shows the business is still struggling and there's no inkling of an improvement soon, it will carry on in a downward trend. However, if there's signs the business is improving, the 52-week low could be close to the bottom (though trends take a long time to reverse). You are better off buying a stock that's risen 20% off its 52-week low than buying at the low. I will discuss this later but a new 52-week low can happen every week. Just because it's hit one it does not mean it can't hit another.

The key is to find growing businesses that are of **good value**, and that possess **upwards momentum**. Once you find and invest in one of these it can transform your portfolio value. You should look to increase your exposure to improving businesses in an uptrend, not deteriorating businesses in a downtrend.

If you do find yourself holding a business that's deteriorating, the best thing you can do is limit your exposure and cut while the loss is small. I have made the mistake of averaging down so many times in the past, and it was generally a result of me being obsessed with the narrative rather than the numbers.

Numbers don't lie – but CEOs can exaggerate and pretend a company is performing better than their income statement indicates. It's in their interest to do so. They are not objective. Numbers are.

Trust the metrics before the management, especially in small companies.

Here's how to handle momentum in action:

Example

Let's say my portfolio is £100,000 and I have made an investment in a company of £3,000, which is 3% of my total portfolio value.

I have a 20% stop-loss in below my buy price, to limit my loss. Then over a few weeks the share price rises by 20%.

What do I do now?

Firstly, I move my stop-loss up to make it a risk-free investment. I can't lose money on this now. There is an exception here: if the company releases truly disastrous news and the share price gaps down, meaning it opens more than 20% below its previous session closing price (but this is very rare in decent companies). So let's say I am 20% up, and I move my stop-loss to my buy price.

The three scenarios that can happen are:

1. **Make a loss:** slim possibility.
2. **Breaking even:** possible.
3. **Making a profit:** probable.

The chances of you breaking even are pretty slim (if it's a company that is fundamentally improving with momentum). So I now have an investment where there's a possibility of breaking even but a probability of making profit.

Having covered off my possible loss on this first investment, I invest another 3% of my total portfolio value again and put a stop-loss 20% below this, to limit a loss there. Therefore risking another 0.6% of my portfolio value (20% of 3%). This may sound complicated – and I do point out a simpler method later – but as long as you record how many shares you buy in a new investment, it's not hard to remember to put a new stop-loss on that same amount of shares. Regardless of which method you use, I would suggest using a spreadsheet for your portfolio management, which I detail later.

Even though I now have £6,000, or 6%, of my total portfolio value invested in this company, my risk is still only £600 or 0.6% of my total portfolio value. Therefore my potential reward has increased while my risk has stayed the same.

My next goal is for my second 3% tranche to rise by 20% to make this part of it a risk-free investment. **I will repeat this process as long as the share price keeps rising.** I use 20% increments because this allows for a little bit of volatility in the share price.

Don't miss out on big winners

No share price goes straight up. After a decent rise it's typical for the share price to come back a little and consolidate. So it's important during this period not to get stopped out and miss out on a potentially bigger long-term profit. Sometimes multi-baggers rise slowly for years. You do not want to take a quick 20% profit to miss out on a 200% one. This return will be even more impressive if the company pays a dividend.

It's pretty much guaranteed that the faster the rise in a share price, the more pronounced the pull back will be when it happens. And, after this consolidation, the share price could rip up even further, experiencing an even bigger rise.

You do not want to miss this. This can happen often. Many investors who had missed the initial rise will be watching with FOMO for any pullbacks. When it falls, many still will not be able to bring themselves to buy – but when it starts rising again, they pile in.

I will talk about momentum again later. It's a very powerful force. Risers attract buyers and fallers attract sellers. At some point you might want to stop moving your initial stop-loss up, because even the very best long-term performers have periods of brutal consolidation. They could experience a 30 to 50% pullback – but go on to do another few 100% rises over the next few months and years.

So, at some point, after you have moved your initial stop-loss to the point when you can only make a profit (maybe 60% above your buy-in price) it would be sensible not to keep moving the stop higher. This way you can only make a profit and you will not miss out on any long-term potential.

I want to be clear here. You should always limit your downside on new investments by 20%. When I say stop moving your stops up, **this is only on investments that are around 60% in profit.**

If the company's operations and fundamentals continue to improve, namely growth is still evident and valuation is not stretched, the share price should continue to rise. This company could turn out to be a superstock you do not want to sell. I will give a real-life example.

Example – a stock market star

From December 2008 to November 2021 **JD Sports Fashion's (JD.)** share price rose by 13,629%.

In the period between December 2008 to September 2009 it rose by 256% and the biggest pullback its share price experienced was just 10%. This is a big fast rise, and it obviously needed a pullback to consolidate.

From September 2009 to November 2009 it experienced a 30% pullback. After this it continued to rise but from June 2011 to December 2011 it experienced a 47% pullback, its share price dropping from 10.5p to 5.6p.

In April 2017 it dropped 35% from 92p to 60p. From September 2018 to December 2018 the price fell 41%. Then in the Covid Dash for Cash Crash it dropped from 177p to 55p, a 69% fall. However, the share price went on to hit a high of 234p in November 2021, a 13,629% rise from 2009. You have to give yourself a chance of capturing these kinds of big returns.

If you continually move your profitable stops up by 20% every time the share price rises by 20%, sooner or later the share price will pull back for a consolidation, and that is likely to mean a drawdown of more than 20%. Meaning you will get stopped out.

With JD Sport Fashion you would have been taken out by the 30% drop in 2009 at 5p and missed out on one of the best performers in the stock market over the last 20 years. My thought is: **once your investment has risen by 20% three times, stop moving your profitable stop-loss up when the share price rises by 20%.**

Here is an example of this in action:

Example

Initial investment:

- Portfolio value = £100,000
- Initial investment 3% of total portfolio value (£3,000)
- Share price = 100p
- Stop-loss = 80p
- Risk = -£600 (-0.6%)

First 20% rise:

- Share price = 120p
- Stop-loss = 100p
- Risk = £0 (0%)

Second 20% rise:

- Share price = 144p
- Stop-loss = 120p
- Reward = £600 (+20%)

Third 20% rise:

- Share price = 173p
- Stop-loss = 144p
- Reward = £1,320 (+44%)

Remember, this is only on an initial investment. You can layer these investments. For example, you could add another 3% of your total portfolio value when your initial investment is at the risk-free stage, i.e. 20% up.

This is where I would leave my stop-loss.

Why?

I do not want to be stopped out of a company whose share price could go on to increase many multiples from my initial investment, just because of volatility. I am not saying you will pick the next JD Sports Fashion, the share price of which rose by 13,629% in 13 years, but even a fraction of this upside could transform your portfolio value.

If a company you invest in rises by 1,000%, £1,000 would be worth £10,000, which is a ten-bagger. You do this another two times and your £1,000 becomes £1,000,000.

JD Sports Fashion was greater than a 100-bagger!

You're probably thinking, *when would I sell such a stock?* Unfortunately, you can't just keep moving your stop-loss up by 20% every time a stock rises by 20% and expect handsome profits. All share prices experience pullbacks and consolidations on the path to outperformance, and one or more of these is likely to be 20% or greater. Always having a stop 20% away means you will only ever capture smaller incremental profits at the expense of a bigger one.

The 20% rule is helpful when initiating a position – and yes, it means sometimes an initial position in a future big winner gets zapped (but, as I explain later, you don't merely forget such companies; you keep watching them, and can initiate another trade when momentum shifts) – but it is not sufficient for nursing winners.

This is why I suggest you relax this practice after you are 60% up. There's no hard and fast rule to this. The goal is to make sure you do not completely lose this profit – but also not miss out on something greater. Sometimes you have to mentally accept that you have a minimum of 60% banked and let the share price do its thing. Having said that, if a share price kept moving up to the point where I was 200% up then I would be silly to just sit there with merely a potential 60% profit. Of course, I would move the stop-loss up – but I would give the share price more room than 20% to allow for greater volatility. This is where charts come in handy. They give you an idea of support and resistance levels where trends can be observed. If a major support level is broken, there's a higher probability a share price may be starting a new downtrend. I discuss charts in chapter 23.

Some investors may be reading this thinking, *60% is not going to make me rich!* Firstly, 60% is an excellent gain. Secondly, some of the best investors have struggled to earn anywhere near that amount over longer periods of time. If you can earn 40% on a yearly basis, the compounding effect of this will provide you with truly exceptional returns. If you start with £10,000 and achieve 40% every year for 20 years, by year 20 you will have amassed £5.9m.

Making sure your stop-losses are not too tight means you are more likely to capture very big gains over the long term by holding a superstock performer.

Remember average daily volume? Monitor the average daily volume to make sure when you add a new position your total holdings aren't exceeding 20% of this, or you will have trouble selling, should you need to sell.

Another way to average up

The above averaging-up example is just one way you can limit your risk but increase your reward. There's a few iterations of this I use. Here's another. Let's say your initial investment into a new stock is 2% of your total portfolio value (so if your total portfolio value is £100,000 you would invest £2,000).

If you average up when this initial investment is up 30%, by **half the amount** you originally invested, you would still be 20% up on your entire investment. Therefore you could still add a stop-loss at your original buy price, making it a risk-free investment. This obviously works for any percentage as long as the second investment is half the size of the first one, which you are 30% up on.

Example

Let's say you invest £2,000 at 100p a share. The share price rises by 20% to 120p, so you raise your stop-loss from 20% below your buy price to your buy price, making it a risk-free investment. If the share price rises to 130p, you would be 30% in profit and your £2,000 would now be worth £2,600.

If you invest another £1,000 at 130p, it will raise your average buy price but you will still be 20% up on the total investment. Therefore you could keep your stop-loss at 100p (you would have to amend the stop-loss to make sure you include all your new shares too) and still have a risk-free investment.

This means you have increased your potential reward because you have invested more – but your risk has remained the same.

If the share price rises again to the point where your total new investment becomes 30% in profit, you can add another £1,500 (half the £3,000 you've invested) and you would still be 20% up. Therefore you can repeat the step above.

Summary

The **how** of portfolio management is an essential skill you need to apply in order to not only make money but to avoid losing money. If you are disciplined about your portfolio management you can avoid most of the issues private investors face. You would be surprised how many of these issues are to do with avoiding losers rather than picking winners.

There's no point buying an excellent heating system for your house if you have old windows and doors with big gaps between their frames and the structure which let most of the heat out. The heating system could be working as hard as possible but your house will never become warm in the winter due to this poor insulation. If you have excellent insulation you do not need the best heating system, you just need one that works; you will not be letting any heat escape.

Keeping with the house theme, portfolio management is like the roof on your house. If you don't have one, or it's full of holes, everything inside the house will get ruined.

Start small, focus on risk first. Think, *how much can I lose on this investment?*, not, *how much can I make on this investment?* Keep your losers small and cut them with a stop-loss set at 20% below your buy price. Average up on your winners. This will ensure your portfolio value is leveraged towards your winners, not your losers.

Part Two:
What

13.
The What to Buy – Fundamental Research

"The stock market is filled with individuals who know the price of everything, but the value of nothing."
—Phillip Fisher

What not to buy

Before I discuss the **what** to buy in my **what, when, how** strategy, it is just as important to know what *not* to buy.

This is because your portfolio value is affected by both winners and losers. So firstly you have to make sure you try to avoid losers. Having said that, it doesn't matter how much you try to avoid them – you will make some investments that go wrong. (So it's important you keep your exposure to these losers as small as possible as I described earlier.)

It's also imperative that you not only know where to find winners but also know where the biggest losers exist in order to avoid them. I mentioned high-risk/high-reward plays earlier. That's exactly what we're not after. And here's what they often look like:

- Small clinical-stage biotechnology companies.
- Oil / gas / resource exploration companies.
- Companies developing their own IP, especially if they are capital intensive.

There is no guarantee that these companies will ever reach commercialisation. They also require a lot of shareholder funds to find this out. The probability of success is usually low.

Here's another analogy. I recently went on holiday to Tenerife and we hired a fishing boat for half the day. Included in our party was my father-in-law, my two sons, Fred (14), Monty (11) and their two cousins Gracie (11) and Oliver (8).

The captain of the boat asked, "What would you like to fish for?" Not knowing much about it, I said, "Fish". He laughed and realised I didn't haven't a clue and said "Small or big ones?".

I asked, "Which is easier to catch?"

The captain said, "The small are easier to catch but if you catch a big one it's more fun."

My sons and their cousins all shouted "Big fish!".

So they hooked up the boat to catch big fish. It transpired that the captain wanted to catch a Marlin because they're fast, athletic and they can be pretty big. The Striped Marlin is the second fastest fish in the world, swimming at up to 50 miles per hour. So to catch one is a badge of honour. What I didn't realise at the time is, it's also very hard to catch one. From the captain's point of view it's also better for his marketing. A picture of a group of people holding a big marlin is a lot more sharable than a few small fish.

We sat on this choppy little boat going up and down this same stretch of water for two hours. At one point the captain got very animated, shouting something in Spanish, but among his words I caught a snatch of English: "Marlin, did you see it? It was on the line."

It got away. Another half an hour passed and the kids were looking thoroughly bored. So I asked the captain if we could switch to catching smaller fish. He looked disappointed but changed all the rods and within half an hour, Fred caught two fish, Monty three and Oliver caught three. The kids were really enjoying it.

What would you opt for?

The question is, would you like to come home with a guarantee of having caught a load of fish, of all different sizes, or are you prepared to go for broke and go for the big ones knowing you may come home empty handed?

When it comes to investing, you have to fish in the water where you know you will get a predictable return with the chance of the odd big one. Not go for the odd big one knowing you might end up with nothing. It's about consistency.

What to buy

What am I looking for?

I am looking for superstocks. These are companies that can be ten-baggers. If you don't look for them you will not find them. Later in this chapter I will introduce you to ten previous superstocks and show how they all share five common traits. If you search for these traits in a company, even if you don't capture a ten-bagger, you are likely to invest in a very good business with very decent upside.

When looking for businesses I to try to categorise them under one of the following headings:

- good
- great
- exceptional.

If they are not in these categories, then they are average or below average and I will avoid them as they are likely to provide me with below-average returns.

Good

A good company is one that is growing, is of good value and healthy – but its margins may not be spectacular, signifying they have a good product or service but it's not particularly unique. They efficiently serve an area of the market, and competition within this sector may not increase if newcomers perceive it as unattractive. At the same time, existing competition means that scaling within this sector could prove difficult.

If average and below-average companies make up around 60% of companies listed, good businesses make up around 25%. So only

25 companies out of 100 can be defined as good. These types of companies are worth monitoring; prudent decisions by management in operations, product or service improvements could potentially transform such firms into great businesses.

Great

A great company is one that is growing, is of good value and has very decent margins, suggesting the company is run efficiently and offers a product or service superior to that of other companies. Additionally, it could be that it is one of only a few companies within its market. Its efficiency and product offering means there is also potential for scale in a market it knows very well. However, such a company may be domestic rather than international.

Again, management decisions could potentially transform such a company – this time into an exceptional business. I would suggest that only ten out of a hundred companies can be regarded as great. This type of business can, over the years, go on to be a superstock.

Two examples I would give here are **Ramsdens (RFX)** and **Time Finance (TIME)**. Ramsdens is a diversified financial services provider and retailer, operating in the four core business segments of foreign currency exchange, pawnbroking loans, precious metals buying and selling, and the retailing of second-hand and new jewellery. The group operates from 169 stores within the UK (including one franchised store) and has a growing online presence.

As far as I can make out, it is one of only two listed businesses operating this type of model within the UK. The other company is slightly larger and called H&T; I prefer Ramsdens, as it is smaller and more efficient. Ramsdens has identified over 300 locations where it could potentially have stores, and is opening around ten stores a year on average. It already has 169 stores, so you can assume it has had plenty of practice of picking the right locations and efficiently opening stores. Rolling out these stores is not particularly challenging for the firm, and it becomes less financially burdensome the bigger it becomes. So it not only achieves growth from existing stores but from new ones, too, and as it becomes bigger its economies of scale improve too. I believe this is a great business because not only is the business profitable on decent margins but it can scale domestically quite efficiently.

On 6 August 2024, Ramsdens released a trading update for the current financial year to 30 September 2024, in which it stated:

> "[G]ood trading momentum has continued into the second half of the financial year to date. This positive performance continues to reflect the strengths of the Group's diversified income streams, the ongoing and successful investments made in enhancing the customer proposition, and the high gold price driving a better-than-expected performance in the Precious Metals segment. As a result, the Board now expects FY24 Profit Before Tax to be at least £11m, which is ahead of its previous expectations (FY23: Profit Before Tax of £10.1m)."

Time Finance is another great business that has continually performed since a new CEO took the helm in 2021 and refocused its core offering. Time Finance provides small and medium-sized UK businesses with flexible funding facilities. It offers a multi-product range concentrating on asset, loan and invoice finance.

High street banks have largely turned their back on UK SMEs so Time has stepped into this niche. It's proving to be a great success, with impressive growth – and it's scalable, too, as they focus on being an 'own-book' lender; which means the more loans they make, the more money they earn (which means they can in turn loan more).

On 27 June 2024 they released a trading update for the year ended 31 May 2024, which showed a 20% increase in revenue to £33.0m, a 38% increase in profit before tax to £5.8m, and own-book lending up 25% to £91.5m (FY 2022/23: £73.4m).

Great businesses – if they continue to scale efficiently over time – can become superstocks or ten-baggers.

Exceptional

An exceptional company is one that is growing quickly, has very decent margins, but also has a market-leading service or product that is globally relevant.

These are rare businesses. I would suggest they make up less than 5% of businesses that are publicly listed. Their value may be regarded as stretched compared to their sector peers – but this is because they are not like their sector peers.

The superiority of their products or services means they deserve a higher rating, because their growth and earnings potential is also a lot greater. It's like comparing a well-paid Premiership football striker to Cristiano Ronaldo in his prime. There are plenty of Premiership strikers – but there was only one Ronaldo; as such, his earning power dwarfed theirs.

I believe an example of an exceptional business is **Beeks Financial Cloud (BKS)**. It is a leading managed cloud provider working exclusively within the fast-moving sector of finance. Its infrastructure-as-a-service model is optimised for low-latency private cloud compute, connectivity and analytics, providing the flexibility to deploy and connect to exchanges, trading venues and public cloud.

Its exchange cloud infrastructure as a service is ground breaking. As a result, it has signed contracts with the two of the biggest stock exchanges in the world, The New York Stock Exchange and the NASDAQ.

This sees these exchanges physically locating Beeks' infrastructure within the actual exchanges. It also means these exchanges sell Beeks' product as a white label to asset managers, banks and stockbrokers.

These potential customers can set up their own trading platforms at the exchange using Beeks' infrastructure in a matter of days to weeks, with little upfront capital expenditure as it's as a service – meaning they can pay as they go. They can also scale these platforms effortlessly. To do this themselves would cost lots of money and take months. Working within finance means it's highly regulated as all data has to be super secure and conform to high standards. To achieve this level of trust from global exchanges is a great barrier to entry. It has taken Beeks three to four years to foster these relationships and it is now starting to pay off.

Beeks has achieved 32% compound annual revenue growth since 2018 and on 22 July 2024 it provided an update on trading for the year ended 30 June 2024. Revenue was expected to be approximately 27% higher than FY23, delivering underlying EBITDA growth of over 27% and underlying profit before tax growth of approximately 67% versus FY23.

In the second half of the year, Beeks continued to achieve a positive free cash flow position in line with management's previously stated strategy, with unaudited net cash of £6.58m at the period end (H1 24: net cash of £5.44m; FY23: net cash of £4.41m).

Exceptional companies have a good chance of becoming a superstock – i.e. a ten-bagger.

A superstock formula

So this begs the question: *Can you create a formula to capture a ten-bagger?*

Looking at the ten superstocks I highlight shortly, I believe it is possible.

I want to make a distinction. Ideally, I want to be invested for years in a company that keeps improving and whose share price keeps rising. I am not talking about trading opportunities, where I will jump in and out for a quick 10–20% on a technical bounce or rally. I am talking about great businesses that possess:

- growth
- good value
- excellent potential.

There's a lot of snobbery about whether people are traders or investors. I used to perpetuate this feeling, too, by jokingly calling people dirty traders – but the fact of the matter is, the only difference between a trader and investor is the time frame, and there's a higher chance of you losing money if you're a trader. This is because the shorter the time period, the more difficult it is to predict the movement of a company's share price. Shares move due to supply and demand. It's impossible to predict whether there will be net supply or net demand for a stock on any one day.

However, if a company continues to grow and is of good value, there's a high probability, over time, that there will be net demand for its shares.

This is how the famous quote from Benjamin Graham came about:

> "In the short run, the market is a voting machine, but in the long run it is a weighing machine."

He means that stock markets in the short-term ebb and flow based on people's emotions and market sentiment, as reflected in the daily net supply and demand of the shares. But over the long term, the truly great companies show their value.

On the subject of time frames, I've had a few people ask me, "Have you ever held a company for years? You only seem to hold shares for weeks or months!"

Firstly, this is incorrect. I have held companies for years – but this is not a goal in itself. My goal is not to lose money and therefore make a consistent profit. Holding a great company for a long time is undoubtedly (as I said at the start of this chapter) a lovely way to do that. But holding something for a long time won't make it great on its own.

Is the point of investing to make money, or see how long you can hold a company for? Is it better to take a small loss or a big one, if an investment isn't working out? Is it better to hold on regardless of how a business or share price performs? If you were given the choice between making 40% in a month or in a year, which would you choose?

Investors should not get hung up on time frames. I will stay invested in a company if the share price keeps performing. If a company's share price went up by 40% every year for the rest of my life, I would hold it until I died.

However, this will never happen. Most businesses go through bad patches when the share price can drop significantly. What you don't want to do is give up profit on that company with the hope it will recover. Because it might not – or it could take a year or more. Having your capital tied up in an underperforming company is inefficient allocation of capital. There are two possibilities here. Firstly, if you are in profit on a company that has done well, make sure you do not lose this profit by using a stop-loss (as I mentioned earlier) – but also do not make it so tight that you might miss the next leg up. Secondly, if you are sitting on a loss then make sure it doesn't get out of hand. This is why my maximum loss on any one stock is 20% of the allocated exposure I've chosen (3% of my total portfolio value).

Superstocks

As I said, my ambition is to find a **superstock**. I define this as a company that can return over 1,000% on an initial investment.

Don't get mewrong: it's not easy to do this, but we do have some clues on where to find them by looking at companies that have previously achieved ten-bagger status.

Even if you research a couple of stocks a day, it's unlikely that you will stumble across one of these businesses very often. You'll be lucky to find one in a year. They are rare businesses.

I liken trying to find one of these companies to that of mining for a big diamond. Yes, you have to sort through lots of dirt before you find a diamond – but you do not go digging anywhere and everywhere. You only dig where you know there's a higher probability of finding diamonds.

One of the most reliable indicators of diamond deposits is the presence of kimberlite, an igneous rock known for containing diamond ore. Why would you look in areas where there is no presence of kimberlite?

While mining for the big diamond, you will find some smaller diamonds along the way that will be valuable. It's similar to seeking superstocks. You will find some very good businesses in that search, so you will still make money even if you do not find that big diamond with its 1,000% return.

Below is a list of big diamonds or superstocks that have achieved ten-bagger status:

- Asos (ASC) was 70p a share in December 2005 with a market capitalization of £70m. Its share price had increased by over 9,907% by 2017, standing at 7,730p at its all-time highs.
- Cerillion Group (CER) went from 133p to 1600p from 2019 to 2024, a 1,100% rise. In 2019 its market cap was £39.3m. On 20 August 2024 it hit a new high of 1945p.
- FourImprint (FOUR)'s share price was 225p in 2012; by 2024 it was 4480p, a rise of 1,891%. In 2012 its market capitalisation was £60m. Today it is £1.5bn.
- Future Plc (FUTR) went from 101p to 3880p from 2016 to 2021, an increase of 3,700%.
- GB Group's (GBG) share price was 16p in 2009; by 2021, it was 950p. That's a 5,500% rise. Its market cap was £18m in 2009.
- Gaming Realms (GMR)'s share price was 4.24p in 2019; by

2024 it was 36p – a 750% rise. (However, it did hit 47p in 2021, a 1,008% rise.) Its market capitalisation was £12m in 2029.

- React Group (REAT)'s share price was 0.165p in 2019; by 2024 the share price was 1.4p, a 748% rise. Although it did rise to 3.5p during 2021 (the Covid pandemic was good business for a contract cleaner), a 2,021% rise. Its market capitalisation in 2019 was £685,422.

- Tristel (TSTL)'s share price rose from 46p at the start of 2014 to 660p in February 2021, a 1,331% rise. At the start of 2014 its market capitalisation was £18.4m.

- Yu Group's (YU.) share price went from 50p in April 2020 to 1290p in February 2024, an increase of over 2,500%. At the time its market capitalisation was just £8.4m.

What do they all have in common?

These companies all had five traits in common. Plenty of other companies have shared these traits and returned multiples of their initial investment – if not quite achieving ten-bagger status.

These traits are:

1. **Revenue:** All these companies generated revenue (unlike a lot of hope, hype, potential stocks).

2. **Growth:** All these companies experienced revenue growth.

3. **Value:** All these companies were of a good valuation.

4. **Momentum:** All these companies' share prices had momentum.

5. **Size:** All these companies' market capitalisation sat below £100m when the journey to 1,000% began.

If you want to capture big winners that rise for years (not weeks or months) you can discount companies that do not fit these traits. Do not go looking for companies that are pre-revenue, that are not of good value, whose share price is in a downtrend, or which are above a £100m market capitalisation. Simple!

But why are those traits so important?

Let's dig into them.

Revenue

You might think it goes without saying that you want to buy companies that are making money, but there are whole branches of trading and investing that aren't concerned with it.

However, superstocks are always those generating revenue. In fact, that brings us onto the next trait, because there's something about that revenue that's important.

Growth

It's vital that the revenue is growing.

All these ten-baggers experienced double-digit revenue growth, largely above 20% for multiple years. Sustainable winners need to be generating revenue – and this revenue needs to be growing, ideally above 20%.

Yes, there are plenty of pre-revenue stocks that can rise quickly – but they can also fall quickly because they do not generate cash. To exist, they need to raise money – usually via an equity fundraise. These fundraisers are invariably done at a discount to the market price and dilute existing shareholders, which has a negative effect on share price momentum.

If you want to hold a company with a share price that can rally for years, you need to look for companies that are growing their revenue. More revenue, if margins are kept at a constant or improve, means more profits.

Value

The average **price-to-sales** ratio of the ten-baggers in this list was 1.2. This is worked out by dividing a company's market capitalisation by its revenue, e.g. £100m market cap divided by £50m revenue means a price to sales of 2. The lowest price to sales was 0.07, the highest was 3.38, and the median was 0.52. The average forecast price to earnings ratio was less than 15.

Due to growth and the companies maintaining or improving margins, their valuations, in the first few years of their rise, meant they were not expensive either. This helped maintain their upward trajectory. (If a company's profits are growing by 20% or more and its share price is doing the same, then the valuation remains the same, because its price-to-earning ratio remains the same. However, if they are growing revenue by 20% or more but their margins improve, their profit will grow by more than 20%.)

It's very important that a company you are investing in is of good value. Companies with a high valuation are a risk (see chapter 18 for a more comprehensive view on valuations). A high valuation means a lot of potential has been priced in and if that potential does not materialise the share will derate, sometimes spectacularly.

Momentum

The share price of every one of the ten superstocks had strong momentum. This means the share price was in an uptrend. You might think, if a company has growth and value surely their share price would be rising?

Nope. You'd be surprised how long a downtrend can persist. Equally a share price could trade in a range for months before it builds enough momentum to move higher. It's a function of share price supply and demand, which is not necessarily linked to the fundamentals of the business.

How do you measure momentum?

I use the 50-day and 200-day moving averages. If you look at the charts of any of these superstocks, an early indication an uptrend was starting was the share price rising above the 50-day moving average and breaking recent previous highs.

Further confirmation was the share price crossing the 200-day moving average. To complete this uptrend, the 50-day moving average crossed up over the 200-day moving average.

There will be dips in the share price, and it's not unusual for a share price to **drop** below the 50-day moving average. This should not be ignored because it may be the start of a downtrend, especially if it's in conjunction with worse-than-expected financial results (for more information on momentum see chapter 23). It's not out of the ordinary for share price weakness to occur before a company releases less-than-flattering news. However, as an investor you may be biased towards a company and choose to ignore the poor news. Don't. If the share price is weak and the news is not good, you have to avoid any emotional attachment to the story. An effective way of doing this is to rely on the objectivity of stop-losses. They will help you either lock in that profit or save you from a bigger loss than you need to take.

Size

Nice and simple: every one of these superstocks started its journey to 1,000% (or thereabouts) with a market cap of less than £100m.

Small is beautiful for investors, because there is much greater room for growth.

The UK MicroCap League

On my website SharePickers.com I have created the UK's first and only MicroCap League. It is a system that ranks companies on the metrics I have listed – as well as a number of related factors.

Growth, value and momentum are the three most important metrics. But they're not the complete picture. Here's some extra info on what else I consider.

Health

Some things can hinder the growth of a company, like its health or efficiency. These are not metrics that have the biggest positive impact on a share price but they can have a negative effect on it.

Therefore all companies in the UK MicroCap League are scored on three different health metrics:

1. net cash or net debt
2. gross gearing
3. current ratio.

Efficiency

Efficiency is important because it not only shows how well a company is run but efficient companies can also achieve higher multiples on their revenue and earnings. A company with margins greater than its sector peers may indicate they have a moat or barrier to entry. In the UK MicroCap League companies are scored on three efficiency metrics:

1. gross margin
2. operating margin
3. return on capital employed.

Potential

I feel potential should be given some weight. When I refer to potential I mean: How much upside do the company's brokers ascribe to the company over the next 12 months? Even though brokers are paid by the company, their research is meant to be independent, so it should hold some weight.

Also brokers who do not produce realistic targets will lose credibility. If you'd like a second opinion on the potential, I also produce my own forecasts based on broker numbers. If the broker target and my target are far apart then it could be a sign that either I don't know how to value the company or the broker is overly optimistic. Either way it's probably wise to be sceptical when researching, if a big discrepancy occurs.

A word of warning: forecasts are just that. It's an attempt to glance into the future, while the numbers for growth, value, health and efficiency are reported facts and momentum is real time. So supposed big potential is nothing without growth, value or momentum.

Also companies that are performing well operationally tend to continue to do well because it's generally a result of them having a good product or service, at the right price, and being guided by good management. This could lead to forecasts (and potential) being upgraded. Therefore the **potential** figure, on the MicroCap League, is worth paying some attention to but it should not be the deciding factor if growth, value and momentum is present.

There are plenty of great little businesses that are opportunities yet to be discovered, and which could go on to be superstocks. If you invest in just one of these companies and use the strategy I outline in this book, you will transform your portfolio value and wealth.

The UK MicroCap League is a list of over 100 companies with the best risk/reward profile and focus on the metrics all these big winners had in common. Among this list are some great businesses and probably big future winners.

There are two types of business

The businesses you need to look for can be put into two categories: **performers** or **recoveries**.

But, on both counts, their financial metrics should be improving.

Performers vs recoveries

When you invest in a company, it's important you define where the business is in its development. Both performers and recoveries can be of good value. The difference between the two is that a performer already has growth, whereas a successful recovery is forecasting growth to come.

Why would you ever go for a recovery play, if growth's already available?

Recoveries, if they play out successfully, can generate significant returns because they are coming from a lower valuation. *But* they are more risky.

Obviously with recoveries there's the condition that the recovery must happen – but if it does, there's generally a very good return to be had.

Let's dig into the two categories in more depth.

Performers

Performers are businesses that tick many boxes. They are companies that are found at the top of the MicroCap League on my website. All or most of their metrics there will be in green. In short, they possess growth, value, momentum, health, efficiency and potential.

They are growing businesses, at good valuations, with good momentum. They release good news on how sales are growing, as well as how margins are stable or increasing. They show every indication that they will continue to perform.

Your portfolio should do well if it contains some of these stocks. They have a very good risk/reward profile, meaning they have decent upside potential due to their continued growth and are not currently overvalued – plus they are healthy, efficient businesses.

So a steady rise should be expected, as long as they keep performing financially. Their share prices may even move aggressively upwards if they release better-than-expected results. This is not unusual for well-run businesses. Good businesses that are performing tend to continue to do well because it's generally a result of them having a good product or service, at the right price, and being guided by good management.

However, there may have been a better time to invest in these companies – just before they started showing decent growth. Depending on their history they may have once been a successful recovery!

Recoveries

Recoveries are businesses that have had a hard time, whether it be down to macro headwinds or internal issues – but which should revert to their former glory.

You have to be careful of investing in a recovery play too early. The actual recovery part can take a lot longer than expected.

A recent survey by EY-Parthenon showed that of the 294 listed companies that issued profit warnings in 2023, 39 of them had issued three or more.

Three or more!

This is why you should never jump into a company just because its share price has dropped significantly, especially if it's directly after they have issued a profit warning.

Profit warnings are like flying ants. They very rarely exist on their own. If you see one there's likely to be others.

If a friend asked you to invest in a business that wasn't listed, would you do so knowing full well its operations were getting worse?

It's imperative to invest into businesses that are improving. When a previously good company issues a profit warning, stand back and watch. It *could* be a **future** opportunity. It's not an opportunity now. Put it on your watchlist, read its future trading updates and set an alert on the chart (I'll show you how to do this later).

As I mentioned previously, it sounds obvious to say this but you are more likely to make money investing in companies releasing news that is exceeding expectations than those issuing profit warnings.

But you would be surprised how many investors jump into companies whose share price drops significantly directly after issuing a profit warning. DON'T DO THIS!

Momentum is a powerful force: it can carry on in the direction it's going for longer than expected.

As with profit warnings, strong trading updates very rarely exist on their own. Once a company's operations show signs of growth by announcing better figures than expected or new contracts, it's not unusual for this trend to continue. It is winning these contracts because its product is good, priced competitively, and the management is efficient at selling it. These factors don't stop overnight. This improvement could be as a result of a major restructuring after a profit warning. This is why recoveries do not happen overnight.

So you are better off searching for companies releasing good news than bad news.

A recovery play is likely to have issued *multiple* profit warnings. This makes current investors and ones that jumped in on the first profit warning lose faith. They sell out, taking the share price and company's valuation down further. By the time the company issues a trading statement suggesting operations have stabilised (and it's not unusual for this to take 12 months or more), it has become a very unloved company and been sold off heavily. This is where the opportunity lies for a sustained recovery because the company's valuation is already priced for another profit warning.

The trick is not to buy a potential recovery too early. You need to buy a business *recovering*, not one about to issue another profit warning. You have to be sure you rely on the financial metrics the company is releasing. Do not base your opinion on what the company is saying. **Figures are FACT, everything else is just opinion.**

There can be many false dawns in a company's share price before it starts to recover financially. Just because you get a sunny day in February, it doesn't mean the summer has started. You are better off being late to a great party than being early to a bad party.

When an underperforming company with a low valuation releases a trading update underlining the fact they are recovering, its valuation will no longer be pinned to its last set of forecasts but new upgraded forecasts, which will suggest it is unfairly undervalued.

So essentially recovery stocks have the potential to become a performer as long as they achieve growth. However, they do not need to become a performer to generate significant returns. Because they have been sold off heavily, even if they revert to mean the share price could move northwards.

The risk lies in how confident you can be that growth will reappear for a recovery?.

A good way to figure this out is to compare whether its growth within its recent trading update or results (especially half-year results) have significantly improved since its previous release.

Trading updates

Companies release **trading updates** before interim and financial results. Keep an eye out for these. This is usually the first time a company will reveal a successful recovery may be on the cards, or confirm a performer will continue to perform.

But a word of warning: trading updates are just a preview or highlights of the results. They only tend to share the best bits of the business's performance. **Be wary if they do not reveal profit or loss figures.**

I liken a trading update to an estate agent's pictures of a seller's house on a property website. They take pictures from the best angles of the nicest parts of the house, using a special camera lens to make the rooms seem larger than they actually are.

To get a proper perspective of the house you have to go and see it. Sometimes you will visit the house and it will look as good or maybe even better than the pictures online – but there are occasions when you feel the photos misrepresent the actual house. I visited a house for sale, after seeing it online, only to discover the garden was a fraction the size of what was portrayed on the website. The estate agent's pictures will also often leave out the worst parts of the house. So when reading a trading update, you have to be aware of what they are *not* saying as well as what they are saying.

Conversely, if a company's last set of final results was good but its recent trading update or interim results are less so, be wary, unless there's some seasonality within its figures which normally means H2 is traditionally the stronger half. If the company states that its results are usually **H2-weighted** (meaning more revenue is generated in the second half of the year) go back to its previous set of results and check if this is normal for its business. If it is not the case, be wary as the business may not perform as well as it suggests. Remember, figures are facts. You have to determine whether what the CEO or company says on video presentations or in RNSs (regulatory news released via the London Stock Exchange) are opinion or fact.

Here are two hypothetical examples showing how opinion and fact have to be sifted:

Company 1

> "Even though the business has shown resilience and performed well in the first half of the year, it is slightly below last year's levels. However, we continue to maintain our focus on accelerating our growth in both existing and new markets and expect our full-year results to be second-half weighted and therefore be in line with market expectations."

Company 2

> "Even though the business has shown resilience and performed well in the first half of the year it is slightly below last year's levels. However, we expect our full-year results to be second-half weighted due to orders received being 23% ahead of levels this time last year. We therefore expect results for this year to be in line with market expectations."

Company 1's statement says it is just hoping the second half of the year will be better. Company 2 has stated that it has received orders that will be 23% higher than the previous year. There's still no guarantee these orders will be fulfilled in the current year, but the fact it has stated the level of orders suggest there's more substance to its comments. It's more believable that results will be in line with the broker targets.

Even so, until these orders are reported in its financial statements, do not believe them to be nailed on.

14.
Size Does Matter

> "A river is honoured for its fish, not its size."
> **—Matshona Dhliwayo**

I focus on small businesses that have room to grow. I will refer to them in this guide as micro and nanocaps.

- Nanocaps: companies with a market capitalisation below or equal to £20m.
- Microcaps: companies with a market capitalisation between £20m and £100m.

Market capitalisation

Market capitalisation refers to the total value of all a company's shares. It is calculated by multiplying the share price by its total number of outstanding shares.

Example: If a company has a share price of £1 and has 50m shares in issue, its market capitalisation = £50m (£1 × 50m).

I would define this as a microcap as it's between £20m and £100m.

Even though I personally focus on micro and nanocaps, this book will be helpful for researching any-sized company.

Why do I love nano and microcaps?

I covered this briefly earlier, but here's a chapter explaining my thinking in detail. I hope I can persuade you of their merits if you're at all on the fence.

14. Size Does Matter

The size of micro and nanocaps, if they possess the desired qualities described in this book, means they have the ability to return you *many multiples* of your initial investment.

If you require a relatively safe annual return of 5–10% then there are plenty of funds available to provide you with this. You might even get lucky and achieve 20%.

However, if you would like to achieve returns higher than 20% then you have to take on a little more risk. This is why risk should be assessed thoroughly, as described previously.

Every year I look at the best-performing companies over the following time periods:

- one year
- three years
- five years.

Sixty per cent of the best performers started with a market capitalisation below £100m.

In the book, *100 Baggers: Stocks That Return 100-To-1 And How To Find Them* by Christopher Mayer, the author suggests there's not many shared traits among the companies that achieved a return of 100× but one of them was:

> "Small is beautiful: 68 percent of multibaggers in the selected sample were trading below a $300 million market cap at their low (they were microcaps)."

(Another interesting one comes later.)

It's worth pointing out here that *100 Baggers* only covered US-based companies, which tend to be larger due to higher valuations. So a company valued at $300m in the states would be valued a lot lower in the UK.

Focus

Logistically just focusing on this sector of the market is also more manageable. There are over 1,000 listed companies in the UK but only 600 companies are below £100m.

If you add another filter like 20% year-on-year revenue growth, this number decreases to 150 companies.

As you can imagine, researching 150 companies is a lot more manageable than 1,000 companies. If you add a valuation filter like price-to-sales of less than two (I cover this later), the number of companies reduces to around 100.

The problem most investors have is not finding a company to invest into. It's knowing what specific company to invest in that will provide the best possible return. This is why it's so important, not to widen your options but to *narrow* them – to find the area you know will most likely produce the best results. **You have to specialise, not generalise.**

Your doctor, who is a general practitioner (GP), does not conduct brain surgery in the afternoon. For this you would go to a specialist, a brain surgeon. A brain surgeon is the best person for the job, if you have a problem with your brain.

In the Olympics, decathletes are not the fastest, they do not jump the highest, the furthest or throw that big cannon ball on a cable the longest distance. The athletes that specialise in these disciplines are the best at these sports.

If you focus your research on a small pool of stocks, which you know produce good returns, you will get to know these businesses. You will learn which are doing well and which are not. You will become a specialist in this field. Specialists outperform generalists in every profession.

It's not about going early

Smaller companies are more likely to provide above-average returns. You need to fish in the smallest pond that holds the fish with the greatest potential. However, smaller companies are more volatile and tend to be riskier, so a robust strategy is needed. It is my intention to find great small businesses that could go on to become superstocks and stars of the stock market.

This is not easy. This may seem obvious, but companies that outperform the majority of the market are rare. They are special businesses.

There are plenty of musicians who make a living selling their music to the public, but there are very few who sell hit album after hit album and fill stadiums around the world decade after decade.

Imagine trying to spot a potential global pop star after they have released just one or two songs. It's a near-impossible task. Even the biggest stars do not have hit after hit – it's their ability to produce a body of work that's consistently of high quality that sets them apart. This is the same with listed companies. It can pay to invest in small companies, but if you go too early and too small, before they are commercial (generating revenue and profitable, or close to it), then it's not only harder to predict whether they will be a success but there's a higher chance they will not be. Many private investors put their money into pre-revenue very high-risk stocks expecting them to become special businesses. The risk is too great and the expected rewards invariably don't play out.

With investing, **you do not have to go early**. You can wait, before you invest, to see whether a company starts showing the traits of a great business. These companies possess a better risk/reward profile.

15.
Always Check the Cash

> "It's not whether you're right or wrong that's important, but how much money you make when you're right and how much you lose when you're wrong."
> **—George Soros**

There are many different types of businesses but they can be basically broken down into two types when it comes to assessing risk. One type of business will, in general, always be riskier than the other.

1. Profit-generating
2. Loss-making

If a company is loss-making, you should break it down into two further categories. Are they:

1. Revenue-generating
2. Pre-revenue

If they are revenue-generating I analyse six metrics:

1. Growth
2. Value
3. Health
4. Efficiency
5. Momentum
6. Potential

You'll recognise these, I hope, as the superstock traits from chapter 13. One warning: when researching loss-making companies, **the most important metric** to look for is **cash**.

Cash is as important to businesses as blood is to humans. If they lose too much of it they will die. With loss-making companies it's imperative you find out the answers to these two questions before investing:

1. How much cash do they have?
2. How long will it last them?

The best place to find this out is on the **cash flow statement** on the company's financial report. This should be looked at for all companies you research, but especially with loss-making firms – and above all with loss-making and pre-revenue companies.

Loss-making and pre-revenue companies generally are not good places to look if you want to find a company whose share price will appreciate for years. They may rise for weeks, or if you're lucky months, but eventually they will come back down due to funding issues. They are not generating monetary value, they are consuming it.

In basic terms the cash flow statement, in a company's financial results, shows the actual cash going into and out of a business over the last 12 months, up to its reporting end date.

Companies have a business year represented by a start date and end date. It can vary, but a lot of companies' start date is 1 January with the end date 31 December for the full year. This means the H1 or half year ends on 30 June.

The cash flow statement is broken down into three areas:

1. operating activities
2. investment activities
3. finance activities.

At the bottom of the statement is displayed the current cash position at the end of the period.

Looking at the bottom section of **operating activities** of the cash flow statement, you will see **net cash generated / used in operations**.

A company is either generating cash or using it. If they are loss-making, they are using it.

In simple terms, if a company has used more cash from its operations over the last 12-month period than the amount of cash it has at its reported period end, then it probably needs to raise more money in the not-too-distant future.

This is unless it has raised money after the period end, which will usually be highlighted in its **post period** summary at the top of its financial report. This often happens, as the company has six months to release its final results after its period-end date. So if its results were from 1 January 2023 to 31 December 2023, these results could be released anytime up to 30 June 2024.

Post-period end refers to any activity conducted after the end-reporting date. For example, if a company's end date is 31 December 2023 but it raised money in March 2024, and released their results in May 2024, this fundraise would be included as a post-period event – but the funds raised will not be included on the balance sheet or cash flow statement.

It's also worth checking news from 31 December up until 30 June to see if the company has raised money (though it's rare it wouldn't include this in its post-period summary).

There is one more exception where a company may not need to raise money, even if it has used more cash in operations during the period than it reported. That's if it clearly states and shows proof that its revenue generation since the period end has increased and its costs have come down in order for it to be generating cash.

Even so, be careful of accepting what a company says as fact, as it may just be opinion. Remember figures are **fact**, everything else is **opinion**.

I've invested in plenty of companies who promise to become profitable by next year, only to fail miserably due to 'exceptional circumstances' or 'one-off non-recurring costs' – i.e. excuses. Unless figures show companies to be profitable, they are not.

If you are invested in a company that states this, you may give it the benefit of the doubt because you want it to be true. But that doesn't make it true.

It's also worth noting that full-year financial reports can be released up to six months after the period end. So if a firm hasn't raised cash post period end, the cash stated in the cash flow statement could be six months' worth of cash burn lower when you are reading it.

How much cash is enough?

If a company states it has £1.2m of cash at period end and it used £1.2m in operations over the last 12 months, it has been burning approximately £100,000 of cash per month. If this burn rate continues, by the time you read its financial statement, six months after the period end, the company only has £600,000 cash. This means it would have to start securing extra funds within the next few months.

To be on the safe side, I like to **make sure a loss-making company has more than 12 months' worth of cash**. So, in the example above, where a company is burning £100,000 a month, I would like to see that it had at least £1.8m of cash when it published its last set of results. This means it would still have 12 months' worth of cash. I would also want it to be hitting a major milestone before this cash potentially runs out. This milestone could be a significant announcement or profitability.

To explain this more clearly, here are two examples. The first is a hope, hype and potential company; the second is a revenue-generating company hoping to hit profitability within 12 months.

Example – cash in a hype stock

Ultra Pharma is a company which claims to have a cure for the common cold. The result of its phase-III clinical trials are due to be released in February 2025. It's 25 May 2024 and you are reading its final results for 2023, which have just been released. Their period ended on 31 December 2023 and you notice the firm lost £7.8m from operations during 2023. If you divide this figure by 12, it will give you an average monthly cash burn.

£7.8m divided by 12 is £650,000 per month.

You look at its balance sheet and observe that it had £11.7m cash on 31 December 2023. If you divide this number by its monthly cash burn of £650,000 it equals 18 months. So 18 months from 31 December 2023 is June 2025. This would take them past their significant announcement. This could present a decent opportunity.

Example – cash in a revenue-generating company

Super Juice is a company that sells energy drinks. It is still loss-making but its sales are growing strongly and it claims it will be profitable within the current financial year, 2024.

It's 5 April 2024 and you are reading its final results for 2023, which have just been released. Their period ended on 31 December 2023 and you notice it lost £2.5m from operations during 2023 on sales of £10m, which grew 20% on 2022. The firm claims to be on track to exceed this growth in 2024.

You look at its balance sheet and notice it has £2.3m of cash. Based on last year's loss, they were burning £209k a month. However, you notice that it lost £1.5m in the first six months of 2023 and £1m in the second half. So it's fair to assume you could divide this £1m loss (in H2) by six months to get a more accurate level of its recent cash burn. This equals £166,667 per month. Over a 12-month period, this would work out at a £2m loss. The company had £2.3m on 31 December 2023.

It seems to have enough cash to cover this loss, plus a 20% uplift on its 2023 sales would means revenue of £12m for 2024. It's a fair assumption this company will become profitable in 2024. Remember, this is just speculation on your part. To be sure you could wait for a trading update on the first six months of 2024, which would normally be a month or so before interim results. Remember, figures are fact – everything else is opinion.

16.
Scoring the Metrics

"I will tell you how to become rich. ... Be fearful when others are greedy. Be greedy when others are fearful."
—Warren Buffett

When researching companies, I analyse the six following metrics (which should be getting familiar now):

1. growth
2. value
3. health
4. efficiency
5. momentum
6. potential.

All these metrics are important, but if I had to prioritise which of these actually move a share price I would say you need to pay particular attention to **growth, value** and **momentum**.

This is not to say the other metrics aren't important. In order to achieve a sustainable rise in a share price, health, efficiency and potential are also vital.

For example, if a company is growing its revenue but has a lot of debt and is loss making it could go from hero to zero very quickly.

Efficiency is also important as a healthy company with good margins means it's generating more cash and therefore likely to be afforded a higher valuation multiple than a peer that is less efficient.

All metrics are important – but some are arguably more important than others. This is why on my website I score each metric on every company I analyse.

The highest-scoring metric is growth, followed by value, then it's momentum and potential followed by health and efficiency.

They all play a part in the performance of a company's share price but some metrics play a bigger part.

17.
Growth

"Once a business is well established, the greatest opportunity for gain is afforded during the period of growth in earning power."
—**T. Rowe Price**

For small businesses, growth is essential. Revenue (or topline) **growth** provides the upside and confirms the *potential* of the business. For small businesses, no metric is more important. This chapter is designed to explain it in depth and show its positive effects in action on the kinds of shares we're looking for, as well as to highlight some importance nuances.

The essential thing

Growth is essential for three reasons:

1. It is commercial validation that the product or service the company is selling is *actually* selling. It's also proof there's increasing demand for its product or service.

2. Every other financial metric is reliant on revenue growth, including value generation.

3. It shows the company is improving.

As I mentioned earlier, you need to be investing in businesses that are improving. Growth is a very good sign this is happening. When companies issue profit warnings, they are generally saying their revenue and/or profits will be less than the previous year.

When companies issue news that's welcomed by the market, resulting in share prices rising, it's invariably growth in their revenue or profits or news that could lead to this.

The less revenue generated, the less potential profit. A company can generate more profit in another way, by cutting costs to improve margins. However, the profit is always tied to how much revenue is being generated.

Example

Let's say a company has the following financial metrics:

Revenue = £10m

Costs = £8m

Profit = £2m

If revenue decreases and costs are the same, there's less profit.

Revenue = £9m

Costs = £8m

Profit = £1m

Even if the company cuts costs, profit is still a percentage of revenue and there's only so many costs a company can cut. Profit is generated from revenue not costs. So pay close attention to revenue generation.

What you are looking for is consistent growth in revenue year over year. As a rule of thumb, double-digit growth is good – but **revenue growth of 20%** or more shows the demand for a company's products or services is meaningfully increasing. If a company grows at 20% per year, after four years it will have more than doubled its sales.

All else being equal (and this is important), if a company can achieve this type of growth its value should double too, usually before year four. This is because the stock market prices in what it can. If it looks like a company's profit will be doubling by year four, the share price will rise to reflect this usually way before year four.

However, if costs are also increasing, be wary: it means the company is sacrificing its margins at the expense of sales.

Here are three examples where consistent sales growth has led to big returns:

JD Sports Fashion (JD.)

JD Sports is a leading global omnichannel retailer of Sports Fashion brands.

JD Sports managed to increase its revenue by over 20% every year from 2015 (£1,522m) to 2020 (£6,111m). This is compound annual growth of over 25%. In that time the share price went from 20p to 166p, a 730% return.

On 31 December 2008 JD Sports' market capitalisation was £130m – a microcap. Now it's a £7.7bn company.

Yu Group (YU.)

Yu Group is an independent supplier of gas, electricity, meter asset owner and installer of smart meters to the UK corporate sector.

Yu achieved revenue growth every year from 2017 (£45.6m) to 2023 (£453m) by a minimum of 39% per year (apart from a 9% dip in 2020 due to Covid, when businesses were in lockdown and used less energy). This is a compound annual growth of over 40%. From 2107 to 2024 its share price went from 60p to 1800p, an increase of 2897%.

At the start of 2018 Yu Group had a market capitalisation of £10.4m – a nanocap. Now it's £270m.

Future Plc (FUTR)

Future is a global platform for specialist media.

Future generated revenue growth every year from 2016 (£59m) to 2021 (£607m) by a minimum of 40% per year. This works out at a compound annual growth of over 40%.

Future's share price from 2016 to 2021 went from 101p to 3880p, an increase of 3.700%. Future's market capitalisation on 30 December 2016 was £80m – a microcap. Now it's £1.2 billion.

Revenue growth alone is not enough

Revenue growth is a very good starting point. But if it's only revenue that is growing, be wary. If all other metrics are not also growing, this means margins are getting thinner. This means less profit to the bottom line for profitable businesses – or bigger losses for loss-making companies.

Unless a company specifically states its margins will be improving going forward, revenue growth alone could be seen as a *negative* – the cost of this growth is economically unviable. What happens if its revenue growth slows? This will have a double impact on the bottom line, because less sales means less profit, and thinner margins do too.

This is why at SharePickers.com I analyse five different growth metrics:

1. revenue

2. operating profit

3. net profit

4. operating cash flow

5. free cash flow.

I also analyse the efficiency of a business regarding its margins and return on capital employed – more on that later.

Growth and value

There's one last but very important point I want to make about growth. A company that only possesses growth without a decent valuation is like a jet fighter plane running low on fuel. (Don't confuse share price and valuation. The share price is a reflection of the valuation attributed to a company – more on this in the next chapter.)

It's like Lennon without McCartney or salt without vinegar or... well, you get my meaning.

What keeps a company's share price rising is the presence of both growth and value. If a company has growth but is overvalued, the future potential is largely priced in. If the company does not deliver on that potential, then the high valuation is not justified – and, like the jet fighter plane out of fuel, the share price will drop quickly.

17. Growth

A company at a good valuation without any growth can remain there for a long time, meaning the share price goes nowhere or the valuation can become even more compelling, meaning the share price drops.

This is why in the MicroCap League, two of the highest-scoring metrics are growth and value. Companies that possess both are scored highly.

I will give you an example of why growth and value are the twin engines needed to boost a company's share price.

Example

Let's look at a pretend company called Two Jets (OK, it's similar to a real company but ignore that). The company has a market capitalisation of £50m and generates revenue of £50m, has net profit margins of 10% and grows at 20% a year (it maintains margins).

Even though, over a period of four years the share price has gained 107%, the valuation remains the same, i.e. price to sales = 1, price to earnings (P/E) = 10.

COMPANY GROWING REVENUE AND NET PROFITS BY 20% A YEAR					
	YEAR 1	YEAR 2	YEAR 3	YEAR 4	YEAR 5
REVENUE	£50,000,000	£60,000,000	£72,000,000	£86,400,000	£103,680,000
NET PROFIT	£5,000,000	£6,000,000	£7,200,000	£8,640,000	£10,368,000
NET PROFIT MARGIN	10.00%	10.00%	10.00%	10.00%	10.00%
PRICE TO SALES	1	1	1	1	1
PRICE TO EARNINGS	10	10	10	10	10
SHARES IN ISSUE	100,000,000	100,000,000	100,000,000	100,000,000	100,000,000
SHARE PRICE	£0.50	£0.60	£0.72	£0.86	£1.04
SHARE PRICE GAIN		20.00%	44.00%	72.80%	107.36%
MARKET CAP	£50,000,000	£60,000,000	£72,000,000	£86,400,000	£103,680,000

Example figures – taking off

If this company keeps growing and holds its margins, its share price can continue to rise and its valuation does not increase. However, if a company continues to grow its revenue by 20% but fuelling this growth means its costs increase, then it becomes more expensive. Let's say its net margin drops by 1% a year, and by year five the P/E is 16.7 times.

COMPANY GROWING REVENUE BY 20% BUT ITS NET MARGIN DECLINES BY 1% A YEAR					
	YEAR 1	YEAR 2	YEAR 3	YEAR 4	YEAR 5
REVENUE	£50,000,000	£60,000,000	£72,000,000	£86,400,000	£103,680,000
NET PROFIT	£5,000,000	£5,400,000	£5,760,000	£6,048,000	£6,220,800
NET PROFIT MARGIN	10.00%	9.00%	8.00%	7.00%	6.00%
PRICE TO SALES	1	1	1	1	1
PRICE TO EARNINGS	10	11.1	12.5	14.3	16.7
SHARES IN ISSUE	100,000,000	100,000,000	100,000,000	100,000,000	100,000,000
SHARE PRICE	£0.50	£0.60	£0.72	£0.86	£1.04
SHARE PRICE GAIN		20.00%	44.00%	72.80%	107.36%
MARKET CAP	£50,000,000	£60,000,000	£72,000,000	£86,400,000	£103,680,000

Example figures – soaring high

So growth is good and could still move the share price – but if the valuation is increasing, too, this jet may start to run out of fuel.

I should make a distinction here between the **value** of a company and its **valuation**. The value of a company (in regards to its market capitalisation) increases with a rise in the share price. This is because market capitalisation is the share price multiplied by the shares in issue. So if the share price increases by 10% then so does its market capitalisation. However, this does not mean a company it's valuation has now increased. As in the example above, if the profit a company generates exceeds 10% growth then the market capitalisation as a multiple of its earnings decreases. So its valuation has become more affordable.

You will often hear pious investors say they are value investors; they seem to shun and look down their noses at growth investors. This is as nonsensical as being a growth investor. You should never just invest in a company because it possesses one trait. Successful companies have both growth and value.

Warren Buffett is often described as a value investor, but he sees value and growth as two sides of the same coin. Buffett wrote the following in his 1992 letter to shareholders in his conglomerate, Berkshire Hathaway:

> "In our opinion, the two approaches are joined at the hip: Growth is always a component in the calculation of value, constituting a variable whose importance can range from negligible to enormous, and whose impact can be negative as well as positive. In addition, we think the very term 'value investing' is redundant. What is 'investing' if it is not the act of seeking value at least sufficient to justify the amount paid?"

In summary, when assessing small companies I want to see growth. Topline or revenue growth is the first metric I look at as all other metrics rely on it. The amount of revenue growth I am looking for is around 20% or more. However, this is not to say I will ignore companies with growth between 10 and 20%, especially if this is an improvement on the previous year.

18.
Value

"All intelligent investing is value investing – acquiring more than you are paying for. You must value the business in order to value the stock."
—**Charlie Munger**

Growth provides the upside but value protects the downside. If a company has growth, its share price can rise – but if the valuation goes up, too, without an increase in profits, then the stock becomes riskier. So both metrics should never be looked at in isolation.

In order to avoid confusion I would like to explain some terminology I use in this book in regards to value. When I refer to the **value** of a company I mean the current market capitalisation. This is calculated by multiplying the current share price by the amount of shares in issue, e.g. a company with a share price of 100p and which has 100m shares in issue would have a market capitalisation of £100m.

However, if I use the word **valuation** then it's usually a judgement on that value of that company based on well-used metrics. If that £100m market cap company makes £10m of net profit then its price/earnings ratio would be 10. This is quite a generalisation, but if this is a growing, healthy company, a P/E of 10 is a decent valuation.

You would be surprised how hard it is to find companies that possess both growth and value. They are rare because if a company has growth, its share price tends to rise in anticipation that it will generate greater value. If the share price does rise, so does the value of the company. For example, let's go back to our company with 100m shares in issue, a share price of 100p and a market capitalisation of £100m. If this share price rises to 150p, its market capitalisation becomes £150m. Does the growth in profit justify this new valuation? If its net profit remains at £10m, then the P/E ratio would increase to 15, making the valuation more expensive. However, if this company says it is on track to increase to £15m net profit, its P/E ratio would still be 10 (£150m divided by £15m) – and still a decent valuation.

So it's important to observe both the growth and the value, in order to make a judgement on a company's current valuation. This is why these two metrics (growth and value) are the first two metrics on the MicroCap League and score the highest when it comes to ranking companies.

If I had to pinpoint the most important metric for a small company I would say growth (chapter 17), but closely followed by valuation (this chapter). This is because a new company that is growing aggressively but with small margins can still experience a share price rise because it is assumed margins will improve over time and therefore value-generation will catch up. What if it doesn't?

I have witnessed quite a few companies whose share prices have rallied strongly based on the fact that it is growing rapidly. On these occasions valuation is often sidelined because fans of the company will point out this company should not be judged by traditional valuation metrics – it's a special company, at the cutting edge of its industry.

It may be cutting edge but in terms of risk/reward, **the higher the valuation gets the less reward is on offer and the riskier the stock becomes**.

The stock may take a while to come back to earth, due to momentum, but it invariably does eventually happen. So do not ignore value.

Remember, companies with very high valuations are riskier. In looking for stocks that have good growth but are of a decent valuation, your risk is less and your potential reward is greater.

Current valuation

A company's current valuation should be assessed in order to work out if it's:

- undervalued
- fair value
- overvalued.

Example

Let's say you pop into a quaint antique shop that has a charming little old lady behind the counter.

You are browsing around when your eye settles on a little painting that seems familiar to you as you're a bit of a fan of the artist. You are staring at the 'Portrait of a Young Man' by Raphael. You know this painting hasn't been seen since 1945 and is valued at more than $100 million.

On closer inspection you are convinced it is the genuine article. So you approach the little old lady behind the counter and ask, "How much is this painting please?"

Depending on the answer she gives you, this painting is either undervalued, of fair value or overvalued.

If she says, "That's £50, dear," it's undervalued (massively so).

If she says, "That's $100m dear," it is of fair value.

If she says, "That's $200m, dear," it is arguably overvalued.

Even though this painting is regarded as a masterpiece, if you intend to make money off it, **you have to acquire it at or below fair value**. The further below fair value you can acquire it, the less risky the reward is.

Sometimes a good business on the stock market can be of fair value or overvalued but the stock market is always fluctuating and a few months later, this company could become undervalued. This is why discipline is needed not to just jump in because a company possesses growth and its share price is rising. Opportunities in the stock market are like buses – they do come along quite often. There's no point chasing after one that has just left your stop. Wait for the next one.

A business that is undervalued and growing has very little of its potential priced in. A business that is of fair value has roughly half of its potential priced in. A business that is overvalued has most of the potential priced in.

This is why, for maximum potential, you need to find growing businesses that are undervalued. Sometimes this could mean investing into a recovery play whose valuation has been hammered due to it missing its previous growth targets. However, when its growth returns, there's usually a lag before its valuation catches up to its new potential.

Finding a company that possesses both growth and good value is rare – but if you do find one, and you've done some research on it, consider investing in it. I say *consider* investing in it because there are other metrics to look at (which I cover soon) but growth and value are two of the most important.

How to value a business

There can be many ways to value a business depending on the type of business it is, but you need to try to value it in order to work out if it's undervalued, fair value or overvalued.

Before you try to value a business you should first work out where the business is in regards to its development.

So first establish what type of company it is. Is it:

- pre-revenue and loss making
- revenue generating and loss making
- revenue generating and close to or at breakeven
- revenue generating and profitable?

Revenue generating and profitable businesses are usually measured on their profit in relation to its market capitalisation (mcap). This is known as the price/earnings ratio (PE), one of the most well-known metrics. A high figure means you are paying a lot for those earnings (which may be fine if future earnings show up at a higher level), a low figure means you are paying less.

Example: if a company's mcap = £100m and it earns £10m, its PE = 10 (£100m / £10m).

What if you are looking at less-established businesses not yet generating a profit?

Revenue generating and loss making companies can be valued on a price/sales (P/S) metric. This assumes, when (or if) the company becomes profitable its margins will be similar to sector peers as they have similar costs, etc.

As an example, if a company has mcap = £20m and sales are £10m its P/S = 2 (£10m / £20m).

If a company is **revenue generating and close to or at breakeven**, a good metric to look at is EV/EBITDA.

EV stands for enterprise value. It is a more accurate way to value a company than the market capitalisation, as EV takes into account debt and cash. In real life would you even contemplate buying a business if you didn't know how much cash and debt it has?

EBITDA means earnings before interest, tax, depreciation and amortisation.

If company A has a market capitalisation of £50m, has £5m of cash and £1m of debt, its enterprise value would be £46m. (£50m - £5m + £1m)

Generally it's a good sign if a company's enterprise value is below its market capitalisation; it means the company has more cash than debt.

Issues with EV/EBIDTA

EBITDA as a measure of profitability attracts a lot of stick from investors who prefer to invest in more mature companies. This is because it's not actual profit. A company can still be losing money but post EBITDA profitability.

So why use it?

Well, for less mature companies, if their EBITDA is growing, it's a good sign they are headed in the right direction – but never assume, just because a business is EBITDA profitable, that it won't need to raise funds. EBITDA profitability does not equate to free cash flow.

EBITDA is earnings before interest, tax, depreciation and amortisation. It can be worked out by taking the operating income and adding back in the depreciation and amortisation. By excluding these items it's felt you can have a better understanding of the cash profits generated by the company's business (because depreciation and amortisation are non-cash costs).

So EBITDA only looks at part of a business's financial story. OK, this part of the business may be important – but so are the parts not included in EBITDA. If a company has a lot of debt then why is it relevant to ignore the interest they pay on it?

If a business is particularly capital intensive, e.g. they manufacture products, then why should you not look at the depreciation of the assets involved in the manufacturing? (Depreciation is an accounting practice used to spread the cost of a physical asset over its useful life.)

For example, if a supermarket business has to buy a freezer unit for frozen food that costs £1m, and it estimates it needs replacing in ten years, it can spread this cost over ten years at £100k per year. But it will need replacing. So showing earnings that ignore this is not a true reflection of costs.

Amortisation is similar to depreciation, but it refers to writing down the cost of intangible assets over a set period of time. For example, patents, trademarks, franchise agreements, copyrights, costs of issuing bonds to raise capital, and organisational costs

So EBITDA should never be regarded as profit – but it is a good metric to observe in less mature companies because it loosely represents the cash profit generated by the company's operations.

If this confuses you, just observe whether EBITDA is growing. All metrics in an improving business should be growing (apart from debt).

How much are you paying for profit?

All valuation ratios based on any type of profitability are basically showing you how much you are paying for a company's profit at the current share price.

If a company has a P/E of 10, you are paying £10 for a pound of profit. Generally, the higher the number the more valuable the market thinks the company is.

So how much should you pay for a company's profit?

To complicate the picture, the multiples investors are willing to pay for company's depends on the growth, margins and sector.

Let's look at an example.

Company A and company B both have a market capitalisation of £100m.

Company A generates £10m in profit and company B generates £5m in profit.

So company A is valued on a price / earnings ratio of 10 and company B is valued on a price / earnings ratio of 20.

So on initial observation you think, 'Company A is cheaper, I'll invest in that.'

But on closer inspection you notice company B is growing at 20% per annum, while company A's revenue has decreased by 10%.

All else being equal company A's profit is 10% less than it was last year but company B's profit will be 20% more.

Which company would you invest in?

The one improving or the one declining?

If this trend continues, by year four company A will be earning £7.3m in profit whereas company B will be earning £8.64m. If the valuation of these companies stay the same, company A would then be on a P/E of 13 while company B would be on a P/E of 11.5, but it is also improving and the stock market tries to price in what's to come.

Investors are prepared to pay a bigger multiple for a high-margin, fast-growing company than a low-margin, low- or no-growth one. It sounds obvious, but growth means more potential profit dropping to the bottom line each year. Higher margins also mean a bigger slice of that revenue gets turned into profit.

Remember, growth is important, it shows a company is improving – whereas lack of growth shows the opposite. So you are better off investing in an improving business than one that is not.

There are odd occasions when a stock can over sell and be due a technical bounce, but nine times out of ten a company that drops dramatically, will drop further.

Why?

Because the reason the company's share price dropped is probably due to bad news they have just released. **This means the business is not performing.**

Investing into a company's shares because they are dropping is like jumping on a bus that is going in the opposite direction to your desired destination.

You'd have more success jumping into a company whose share price rises dramatically on good news. Something is going right with this business. They are like a bus, going towards your desired destination, heading in the right direction.

Valuing a company on its assets

The examples just given were based on valuing a business on its sales or profits. There is another way to value companies (don't worry, I will summarise what to look out for later): on their assets.

When you look at the balance sheet of any company there are **assets** (what a company owns) and **liabilities** (what a company owes).

If you subtract the liabilities (what a company owes) from the assets (what a company owns) you are left with the company's **net assets**.

If a profitable company is valued at or below its net assets, it could be undervalued. If a profitable company is valued at or below its net assets and it's growing, there's a high probability it's undervalued.

Essentially what this means is, even if you sold all the company's assets off (after paying off the liabilities) they would still be worth more than what the market currently values it at.

It's not that unusual for a loss-making company, not growing, to be valued below its net assets because over time its assets, specifically its cash, will be decreasing.

However, if you find a profitable company that is growing and is valued below its net assets, it's undervalued. This is because the value of its assets are growing but the market doesn't believe it or appreciate it.

It's very rare to find these companies. I managed to find and invest in one at the back end of 2023. It was called **Good Energy (GOOD)**. It had been sold off heavily during the bear market. Its net assets per share was around £3 yet its share price was £2. Its market capitalisation was £30m but it had cash of £24m and was profitable.

I made over 60% profit on it within six months but just after I invested at around £2 the share price dropped to around £1.60 and I thought, 'Am I working this out correctly? Why is this not valued more highly? I must have something wrong.' Then over the next 100 days it rallied by 150%.

In summary, the valuation of a company is very important in relation to whether a share price of a company will perform – and perform sustainably. It's difficult to generalise on what a good valuation for a company is because it's influenced by many factors – its industry, its growth, efficiency, peers' valuations, total addressable market and its position within that sector, etc. However, whenever I start conducting a review of a new company, I will do a quick calculation of its market capitalisation in relation to its revenue, then weigh up its market capitalisation in relation to its net profit. Next, I will check the cash and debt of a company to work out its sales and profit in relation to its enterprise value.

Usually, these multiples would make me interested:

- market capitalisation less than twice its sales
- a P/E ratio less than 20
- an EV/EBITDA of less than 15.

Of course, this is already assuming the company possesses decent revenue growth.

19.
Hope, Hype, Potential

> "Hope is not an investment strategy. Hope is a component of a healthy state of mind, and the opposite of negativity that we see all around. But then, when it comes to the stock market, hope is dangerous."
> **—Anon**

Hope, hype, potential is a term I use to classify a certain type of stock. These stocks are normally small, pre-revenue and loss making but possess big upside potential, which in turn fuels the hope of achieving this goal, which in turns fuels the hype around the company.

A word of warning that most private investors who only invest in loss making, hope, hype potential stocks should heed: if you want to achieve long-term sustainable gains, these types of companies should not dominate your portfolio.

They tend to pop and drop.

Investing in high-risk/high-reward stocks is largely an unprofitable exercise. You may get lucky now and again but the risk on many of these companies is too high for the possibility of them achieving the expected reward.

Think about it in terms of the cheetah and the gazelle. We all know the cheetah is the world's fastest land animal. They can reach speeds up to 68 miles per hour and yet they only have a 10% success rate in catching gazelles, who can only run up to speeds of 50 mph (I say only).

This is because a cheetah can only run at its top speed for 400 yards. Gazelles are able to run for ten times that distance (5,468 yards) at top speed. Overall, a cheetah's kill rate is around 58%, barely about even odds. Whereas African wild dogs, because they hunt in packs and have better endurance, have a kill rate closer to 85%.

I know a cheetah is a stunning-looking animal and is famous for its speed, but when it comes to investing you need to be more like an African wild dog in regards to consistency (not looks).

All that said, it's OK to invest in these stocks sometimes. But you need to be conscious that's what you're doing. You're looking for a pop – not a long-term buy. (For reasons we've covered already, I think that makes them less attractive anyway.) The issue with hope, hype and potential stocks is that some private investors do not use the story to make money; they start believing in the story. So when they are holding a microcap stock that takes off and they find themselves sitting on a nice profit, they do not lock it in. They fall for the hope, hype and potential of the story.

Don't believe the hype, use it to make profit.

Some of my worst investments were because I believed in the story, rather than just paying attention to the numbers. Interviewing CEOs was probably one of the main reasons for this. It's in the CEO's interest to make the story sound positive. They are not giving an objective point of view. A good CEO is part salesman and can be very endearing. I often gave these types of CEOs the benefit of the doubt even though they'd failed to hit previous targets they'd set or their company's financial performance was below par. You will find CEOs of pre-revenue hope, hype, potential stocks are more prone to exaggeration specifically because their fundamentals are not good.

For this reason, pre-revenue companies are largely a false economy that never achieve their potential. You can achieve big gains – but you are more likely to achieve big losses that will outweigh the gains. I see private investors pump these all day long on social media and I know for a fact they are losing money. I can only come to the conclusion that there's only two reasons they keep investing in these junk stocks:

1. They are in denial about losing money

2. They are addicted to gambling

If you want to make money consistently from investing, you should not dedicate more than 5% of your total portfolio value to pre-revenue stocks.

Without a shadow of a doubt, the best-performing companies over longer periods are revenue generating, profitable businesses which possess growth and good value.

However, hope, hype and potential are very powerful forces. They are intangible and not often linked to the reality of what will play out – but that does not stop some of these hope, hype, potential stocks achieving some breathtaking almost stratospheric rises.

Pre-revenue companies should possess huge upside potential but with very little of that potential priced in. Because they are all about hope, hype and potential.

Even a conservative share of their potential total addressable market should give you a path way to a potential ten-bagger. Not that they are ever likely to achieve this; it's the perception that they could achieve this that drives the share price.

Hope, hype, potential

In general to be a successful **hope, hype, potential** company, a company's market capitalisation needs to be £20m–30m to enable it to scale before proper commercialisation and revenue generation happens, because that is when they get valued on real metrics like price / sales. When this happens, they generally disappoint. I've yet to witness a hope, hype, potential stock live up to its potential once commercialisation starts.

The reason pre-revenue stocks can experience a stratospheric rise so quickly is all down to opinion, rather than figures. They are all about the narrative, not the numbers. **Way before they start delivering numbers, it's time to get out.** Hope and hype are more powerful forces than reality. The dream of what can be is more powerful than what will actually be.

No one likes to accept it but the dream of winning the lottery is more hassle free than actually winning the lottery. Your dreams of having millions does not incorporate having to move away from your neighbours, or your friends treating you differently because you now have lots more (unearned) money. Before a lottery win, you were one of them. You experienced the same financial pressures. You could whinge about the price of energy, mortgage payments or car insurance. After the win, you can't. You do not relate to these issues, you are immune to them. Even if you sympathise, it will be seen as fake.

A recent study of the Dutch Postcode Lottery focusing on large lottery wins found little evidence that lottery wins affected people's happiness in a statistically significant way.

If you think you've found an excellent hope, hype, potential stock make sure it has cash. Again, the two most important questions to ask yourself before investing in a loss making company is:

1. How much money does the company have?

2. How long will this cash last?

Funding should not be the story. If it does become the main concern then it detracts from the hope, hype and potential.

With any hope, hype, potential company the potential decreases as its value increases. If you are invested in a pre-revenue loss-making company valued higher than £100m, you've missed the initial hype-fuelled stratospheric rise.

Every time a company doubles in price it becomes twice as difficult for them to double again. This is why hope, hype, potential stocks have to be small before they start their run.

Every portfolio has room for a hope, hype, potential stock as they can dramatically increase the value of your portfolio in a short period of time, *if* you get it right.

I have had three ten-baggers in hope, hype, and potential stocks, namely **Versarien (VRS)**, **EVR Holdings (EVRH)** and **Asiamet Resources (ARS)**.

Where are they now?

Versarien is on the edge of going bust, EVR Holdings became Melody VR which acquired Napster and delisted but its shares cratered. Only Asiamet Resources seems to have any potential left but its shares are currently at 0.76p. I bought them at around 1.2p and they rose to 14p.

Example

Another hope, hype, potential stock that failed to live up to its commercial promises was a company called **Bidstack (BIDS)**. It listed on AIM in September 2018 and the share price opened at 6.6p.

I and others found this to be a very exciting company because its advertising technology could be inserted into computer games in naturally occurring environments. For example, the adverts around a football pitch in the *FIFA* games could be real actual adverts paid for by companies. This was a lucrative untapped area of the market, where advertisers could get their brand in front of hard-to-reach but engaged audiences without spoiling the enjoyment of a game.

By January 2019, the share price had dropped to 4.5p but the CEO was talking a good game about the potential for the company and alluding to possible deals that could be struck with big gaming companies.

I bought in at around 5.5–6p as the company started to release news on a contract with Codemasters, an AIM-listed award-winning video game developer and publisher. Bidstack was to provide native in-game advertising within two of Codemasters' titles, beginning with *DiRT Rally 2.0*, the sequel to the successful BAFTA-nominated *DiRT Rally*.

It also created an advisory committee that included Pete Beeney (Spotify) and Joel Livesey (The Trade Desk). By April the share price had risen to 20p. Then there was speculation over a fundraise, which took the stock down – but I reasoned this was an opportunity to top up because we were in a bull market; interest rates were low, so there shouldn't be a problem landing the investment they needed. Once it was done, I believed the stock would keep powering upward on hope, hype and potential. But remember, once funding becomes the story, the hope, hype potential story takes a backseat.

In May 2019, it announced a £5m fundraise at 12.5p. I remember it happening because I was in Center Parcs, standing at the side of the pool in the pouring rain watching my sons on an Aqua Jet session.

As soon as the market opened, I was on my phone buying as much stock as I could get a quote for. Now the funding had been secured, it would no longer be a concern and the hope, hype and potential would again become the focus for investors. Around 15m shares got traded that day and the share price closed at 14.06p. By 6 June the stock closed at an all-time high of 37.5p. Its market capitalisation was around £80m.

In the meantime Bidstack kept announcing more gaming legends were joining its advisory committee, and it signed deals with Epic Games, Trade Desk and a Milestone Advertising Trading Agreement commencing on 1 January 2020 that saw them agree terms for gross media expenditure up to £10,000,000 per annum for the next two years.

Off the top of my head Bidstack's brokers had forecast its first-year revenue coming in at either £3m or £5m. Whichever it was, it seemed a promising start for a new tech company in a new sector. However, this would not justify an £80m market capitalisation so I was wary even while there were rumours it could exceed these targets.

I had around £420k invested and was sitting on a decent profit so I started putting several stop-losses in at around 10% below each other. There wasn't enough liquidity to sell all my holdings in one go.

Before Bidstack released its interim results, up to 30 June 2019, on 30 September half of my stop-losses had already been filled. Its results showed revenue of just £26,692 against a loss of £1.8m.

The final few of my stop-losses got taken out before it released a trading update on 18 December 2019 stating:

> "The Board is pleased with recent progress and expects that its industry relationships will deliver a material uplift in revenues in 2020. However due to commitments previously anticipated to be recognised in 2019 having been delayed, it is clear that the Company will not now meet its revenue targets for 2019."

The stock started tanking. It consistently missed broker forecasts and racked up big losses. The company recently filed for administration.

So I guess you can conclude that generally hope, hype, and potential stocks never really fulfil their true ambition. The trick is to get in before the hope, hype, potential is anywhere near priced in.

Example

The most recent hope, hype, potential stock I invested in was a company called **Destiny Pharma (DEST)**. I bought it at around

33p and sold half my stock at 65p and the rest at 62p. Average brokers' targets were 165p (350% higher than the current share price).

Did I think it would get there?

I thought it could – but there was a lot of commercial execution risk ahead. And I was not going to reject a 95% gain based on hope, hype and potential taking it further.

As I write this the share price has tanked by over 96% from 79p to 2.25p within a few months, and the firm has announced it is going to delist from AIM.

I made approximately £95k profit on this stock but recently had a sarcastic comment on my YouTube channel saying, "This was a good investment!" This is exactly why you should learn to do your own research. I suspect this person invested in this company after watching a video where I mentioned it. I have no idea when he watched the video or at what level he decided to invest. He could have been buying when I was selling. Hence his animosity towards me. He probably lost money but I made money. It was a bad decision for him but a great one for me.

However, never believe or fall for the hope, hype and potential. Just use the momentum to make a profit. In order to do this you have to lock in this profit using stop-losses. Do them for real. I have heard people say they use mental stop-losses, saying they know where they will get out. **Never do this.** When a stock starts dropping and you have to take action, your emotions are invested and they will cloud your judgement.

Pop and drop

I've seen hope, hype and potential share prices pop by over 1,000% in a few trading sessions and drop by more than 90% over the next few days. The trouble is many private investors tend to invest just after the big rise has happened.

Regardless of how much you believe in the story, if a hope, hype potential stock pops by over 100% it will, sooner or later, drop.

Have a plan for this drop. Put stop-losses in and stick to the plan. You will not think clearly when a share price is under pressure. You are more likely to try to wait for a bounce, which might never come before wanting to hit the sell button. The result is, you will be making one of the most common mistakes private investors make. You let your losses become too big.

As I said, there is room in most people's portfolios for a hope, hype potential stock. But don't fall for the story. The positive momentum the stock experienced on the way up can be equally or more powerful on the way down.

If you are sitting on a profit larger than 20%, make sure you never lose money on them. Put a stop-loss in at your buy price.

Having said this, pre-revenue stocks can be very volatile and therefore stop-losses may not be effective in protecting you. This is because many of these companies' valuations are story-based (as opposed to financial). If the story does not go to plan the share price can move too dramatically for stops, especially if the outcome of the story is negative.

The outcomes of these stories can be binary, so it's either really good or really bad. Some examples of binary plays are clinical-stage biotech stocks or oil/gas explorers. If a biotech company does not achieve its desired endpoints on clinical trials its share price can drop by much more than 20% in one session. This would render your stop-loss ineffective. This is the same with oil/gas explorers. If one announces that it has failed to find a commercial discovery after a drilling campaign (and this happens more often than not) the share price will tank.

I mentioned earlier my experience of a binary outcome investment, which I was sitting on the wrong side of. **Polarean (POLX)** had passed two phase III trials and brokers suggested it had a 90% chance of achieving FDA approval for its medical imaging technology. The FDA issued it with a 'Complete Response Letter', meaning it didn't get approval. The shares dropped by 65% in one day.

Be careful investing in companies with binary outcome stories: if it does not go the way you want, you will take a big hit. The way to play these story stocks is to de-risk before the binary event happens. The share price of Polarean rose by over 500% in the three years I held them but I did not sell one share until it was too late.

20.
Health

"The greatest wealth is health."
—Anon

As I've mentioned previously, there are some metrics that are more influential on the movement of the share price than others. However, as with humans, you should never take your health for granted. Of course, we do. It's only when health becomes a serious issue that we tend to pay attention and try to do something about it. By this stage, it can be too late. The damage is already done.

This is the same with companies. Every company you invest in should be given a health check before you deploy your capital into it. You do not want to be alerted to the health of the business only when it's having an adverse impact on the share price.

Whenever a company I am watching issues interim or final results, I run the figures through my spreadsheets, essentially giving it a health check twice a year. In fact, the companies I monitor receive more health checks than I do.

If a company doesn't have a healthy balance sheet, it can struggle to attract investment. A distinction has to be made between these two types of businesses again: **profitable** vs **loss-making**.

However, in both instances it all comes down to cash, or lack of it. With profitable companies, they may be making money – but if they have a debt pile so large that their profit does not service this debt, they are slowly (or quickly) drowning.

It's like a boat taking on water at a rate of ten litres per minute and all you are able to bail out is five litres a minute. The boat is still taking on a net basis of five litres of water every minute. It's only a matter of time before the boat sinks.

There are three metrics I pay attention to when it comes to the health of a company:

1. Net cash or net debt.
2. Gross gearing.
3. Current ratio.

Net cash or net debt?

As I've mentioned before, cash is the most important metric for any company, it's like blood to a human. If you lose enough of it you die. When evaluating the health of a company, the first thing you should look at is its cash position.

Most pre-revenue companies will have no debt, as in bank debt, but they may have **convertible loan notes**. This is because they are unable to pay back bank debt due to them generating no revenue, however they can pay back loans with equity.

A quick note on convertible loan notes. They largely come from two different sources. If the source of these convertible loans is a company that specialises in convertible loans notes, that firm can crater the share price. This variety has often been termed *death spiral financing*. This is because the creditor has no alignment with other shareholders. All they want to do is get their money back. So they will convert their loan into equity and dump their shares without any regard for the share price. Depending on the terms on the notes they can generally convert their shares at a discount to the market price. This in turn pushes the share price down and they convert more at a discount. Hence the death spiral. The only opportunity here for a trade is when a company announces the termination of the loan agreement, usually via an equity placing. It's a risky play but the share price has been suppressed due to the constant selling. When this selling ceases the share price can act like a coiled spring.

If the source of the convertible loan notes is a board member or a current shareholder, then it's a different story, as they are aligned with current shareholders. So they have loaned the money to the company to benefit the company, not themselves. Therefore it's not in their interest to trash the share price.

Back to cash. If a company is pre-revenue or losing money, as I've mentioned before you have to find out the answers to these two questions:

1. How much cash do they have?
2. How long will this cash last them?

Ideally this cash should give them a runway of 12 months or more.

If the company is profitable, check to see whether the company has debt and whether that debt is manageable. The balance sheet (or **financial position** as it's now called) is where you find out if a company has debt. The balance sheet consists of two parts: **assets** (that which the company owns) and **liabilities** (that which the company owes). Under liabilities, there's two sections. *Current* liabilities have to be paid within 12 months and *non-current* liabilities which don't have to be paid until after 12 months. There could be debt on both, either or neither of these sections. Typically, debt will be described as 'interest-bearing loans and borrowings' or something similar.

Below I show the three metrics I look at to work out whether a company is in a healthy state in regards to debt and other factors. The ideal position for a company to be in is a **net cash position**, which means they have more cash than they have debt.

Example

If company A has £5m in cash and £3m in debt, it has a net cash position of £2m. If it had £3m of cash and £5m of debt it would have £2m of net debt.

If it is in a net debt position, i.e. more debt than cash, then you have to work out if this debt can be serviced. By this I mean can the firm comfortably pay the interest on the debt and maybe even some of the principal (the amount loaned).

Another health metric worth paying attention to is current ratio.

Current ratio

The current ratio, also known as the working capital ratio, measures the capability of a business to meet its short-term obligations due within a year.

The ratio is calculated by dividing the company's total current assets by total current liabilities.

Current assets are short-term assets, such as cash or cash equivalents, that can be liquidated within a year or during an accounting period. Current liabilities are a company's short-term liabilities that are expected to be settled within a year or during an accounting period.

Example

If a company has £100m of total current assets and £50m of total current liabilities, the ratio would be 2 (£100m divided by £50m).

Any ratio over 1 is seen as healthy. If the ratio falls below 1, it means the company has fewer current assets than current liabilities and it may struggle to meet its current liabilities in the coming months.

Gross gearing

Gross gearing is a measure of a company's financial leverage also known as **debt to equity**. It is calculated by dividing its total liabilities by stockholders' equity (or net assets).

The gearing ratio shows how encumbered a company is with debt. On the website I score the ratio into three metrics. Gross gearing below 33% is regarded as healthy and coloured green. Between 33% and 66% needs further investigation. Above 66% is higher risk and coloured red.

21.
Efficiency

> "If you find three wonderful businesses in your life, you'll get very rich."
> **—Warren Buffett**

When searching for potential winners, I state that growth and value are the most important metrics. In regards to growth, I do not want you to believe only topline growth is important. It is important – but this growth needs to be achieved on every level of the income statement.

The ten-baggers I covered earlier on did not only achieve growth in their revenue, but this translated into profit growth at a similar or accelerated rate, due to efficiencies either driven by good management, economies of scale or both.

If a company grows its revenue by 20% in a year but its profit goes down by 20%, then – unless the company had suffered some one-off costs – this extra income is close to worthless. It has cost them to grow that revenue.

This is the opposite of what should be happening. The profits should be growing at least at the same pace as the revenue. If a company achieves 20% revenue growth and its profit increases by more than that, it's showing increased efficiency. It proves the company can scale efficiently.

A company at a decent valuation that grows both its revenue and profit margins is the perfect combination for a positive share price re-rating.

Example

Let's compare two different companies, company A and company B. Both companies are the same size, a £50 million market capitalisation, and both grow their revenue by 20% a year for five years, starting at £50m. By year five this revenue is £103.68m. They are sector peers so both are valued on a price to earnings ratio of 10.

Company A's net margins are maintained at 10%, whereas company B's net margins increase by 2% every year.

Therefore by year five the net profit earned by company A is £10,368,000 whereas the net profit earned by company B is £18,662,400.

If they are still valued on 10 times these earnings, then the market capitalisation of company A would be £103,680,000 whereas the market capitalisation of company B would be £186,624,000. So company B's market capitalisation is 80% higher. Assuming neither company issues more shares, company B's share price would also be 80% higher.

This is why on the MicroCap League feature on my website I monitor not only the growth of companies but their margins, to make sure the growth is being achieved efficiently.

Management

Very good businesses are efficiently run. There's two parts to that sentence. "Very good businesses" are "efficiently run".

A good business can be inefficiently run but still grow and make money. Conversely, if a bad business is run inefficiently it will probably go bust.

So can a bad business be run efficiently? Probably, and that's what stops it going bust. The management can be good but that does not particularly mean the business is. There are plenty of successful, well-regarded entrepreneurs who have had multiple business failures. Would they blame themselves, the economic environment or the business model?

Warren Buffett famously said:

> "When a management with a reputation for brilliance tackles a business with a reputation for poor fundamental economics, it is the reputation of the business that remains intact."

21. Efficiency

Some investors pay close attention to the management. This is never a bad thing to do because a quality management team can make good capital decisions about how to invest company resources. But I prefer to keep an eye on the figures because these are mostly a *result* of management decisions.

Management can make all types of positive soundings about the prospects of the company but unless it's reflected in improved figures, it's just hot air. If a business model is flawed it can never be a market leader regardless of what the management does. So I give figures more prominence than the management.

I have fallen for a positive CEO's vision many times. I have interviewed over 400 CEOs in the last five years and there were times I spoke to a CEO who was so adept at selling their vision that I bought it. Writing it here sounds absurd but the weapons of hope, hype and potential are powerful forces when brandished by an eloquent orator.

After all, cult leaders build their following on nothing more than opinion and vision via the spoken word. When they tell their flock that the world will end they do not have fact or proof on their side, and yet their followers not only believe them but are willing to die for their leader's opinion.

You may think I am going off topic or being a bit extreme here but there are some stocks followed by crowds of faithful followers that only believe the CEO's opinion, disregarding any negative news or price action as just a temporary part of the plan.

I will keep repeating this, but trust the facts, i.e. the figures, not the opinion or the narrative. The figures are the truth 99.99% of the time. Yes, 0.01% of the time there's a crooked CFO massaging the numbers but that's an acceptable risk, and it can be managed by portfolio management.

It doesn't matter how good the management is, if the business opportunity or economics do not stack up there is a very limited positive effect the management can have on them.

Keep an eye on the figures.

All that said, there is one quality worth looking at when it comes to management – and that's the skin they have in the game. Proving my point, this means relying on cold hard figures again.

It never ceased to amaze me, after interviewing a CEO – who was effectively trying to sell his company's shares to private investors – when I discovered that they held very few shares. Be wary of this. There's a difference between a business founder/owner and a manager brought in to run a company in return for compensation.

You usually find business founders/owners live the business and have significant skin in the game. Creating a successful business, for them, is more than just about remuneration. It is not a temporary job, it's about their reputation and legacy. Whereas managers, of course, want to make a success of the business – but there's less at stake if it doesn't work out. It is literally a paragraph on their CV.

In the book *100 Baggers*, Christopher Mayer found one other striking commonality among companies that returned investors 1,000% or more:

> "There was often a large shareholder or an entrepreneurial founder involved."

So pay attention to companies that not only fit the growth and value metrics but who are run by founders. If you want to check whether the directors of a company hold shares in the business it's relatively easy to do, as it will be in their audited full-year results. All listed companies will have an 'investor' section to their website. Once you find this, navigate to the 'financial reports' and open the most recent release. At this point I will usually use ctrl+F on my keyboard and type in the name of the CEO. This will then allow you to see all mentions of the CEO's name, including the part of the report that shows their salary and shareholding plus any options they have.

Bear markets and previous winners

Bear markets force companies to become more efficient or go bust. Generally during economic downturns, the strong get stronger and the weak die, which creates a bigger market opportunity for good businesses.

So when a previous market leader takes a hit in a downturn, keep an eye on it. This is very different to investing in a newer smaller business. Mature, previous market leaders have a proven business model and plenty of customers. They are also probably quite profitable but are making improvements to their business model, in a downturn, to make it more efficient.

Add to the mix that many of its smaller competitors could go out of business and not only has this market leader become more efficient but there's a bigger market share up for grabs.

How to measure efficiency

I look at three metrics to measure efficiency:

Gross margins

The gross margin is the gross profit a company generates as a percentage of its revenue.

To understand why gross margins are important you first have to understand what the **cost of goods sold** means, as this impacts the gross margin.

Cost of goods sold (COGS) refers to the direct costs of producing the goods sold by a company. This includes the cost of the materials and labour directly used to create the goods.

Imagine if two competing companies are selling a very similar product but one's gross margin is higher than the other. It's a more efficient business and would have an advantage over the other. This is because they are managing their labour and supplies in the production process more effectively and efficiently.

The bigger the gross margin, the more profit can drop to the bottom line. Gross margins can vary depending on the sector. More capital-intensive companies manufacturing things like cars or machinery would have a lower gross margin than a software company.

Operating margins

As the name suggests, operating margins represent operating profit as a percentage of revenue. The operating margin measures how much profit a company makes on a pound of sales after paying for variable costs of production, such as wages and raw materials, but before paying interest or tax. It's a measure of how efficient its core operations are. Obviously higher margins are considered better than lower margins, and can be compared between similar competitors but not across different industries.

Generally speaking, this is where the bulk of most costs reside like administrative expenses, or admin expenses, or all costs of a business that aren't directly related to manufacturing, production or sales. In most instances, they're regular expenses that allow companies to continue to operate, which is why they're also known as 'overhead'. So if a company is generating an operating profit it's a positive sign.

Return on capital employed

The return on capital employed, or ROCE, measures how effectively a company uses its total capital employed to generate income. It is calculated as the **operating profit** divided by the **capital employed**.

Capital employed is fixed assets plus working capital or, put another way, it's total assets minus total current liabilities. Current liabilities are a company's short-term financial obligations like bills that are due within one year or within a normal operating cycle. So working capital is all assets minus these liabilities.

Return on capital employed is displayed as a percentage and as a general rule of thumb, a score above 10% shows a company is generating a good return on the capital it is investing.

Let's say company A generates an operating profit of £15m. To work out the ROCE you have to calculate its working capital. On the balance sheet you look at the company's total assets and subtract the company's current liabilities (as these have to be satisfied within 12 months). If, for example, company A's total assets are £200m and its current liabilities are £50m, then its working capital = £150m. You then divide the £15m operating profit by £150m and multiply by 100 to get the percentage. £15m divided by £150m = 0.1 multiplied by 100 = 10%.

22.
Potential (Reward)

"If you invest nothing, the reward is worth little."
—**Anon**

The power of potential

Reward, as I explained earlier, is a metric private investors focus too much on, usually at the expense of the more important metric: risk. Nevertheless, when you invest in a company it is important to not only work out the risk but also the potential reward. If there's very little reward on offer, *there's very little point investing in a company.*

Reward is inextricably linked to a company's current valuation. Potential is the difference between a company's current valuation and what the valuation should be or could be. So, firstly, you have to work out whether the current valuation has priced in the expected potential or not.

Plenty of good listed businesses are not cheap. Much of their potential has been priced in. The trick is to find a good business where the potential is not priced in.

Predicting the future

Share price movement is a lot more about what is going to happen than what has happened. Nobody can tell the future, but with certain types of companies – e.g. mature businesses with predictable revenue streams – it's a lot easier to predict what is likely to happen. This is why large rewards are unusual in large caps.

With less mature, smaller companies the reward or potential can be less predictable, which can be a positive or a negative. It's possible a smaller company can release unexpectedly good or bad news, which will move the share price significantly. This unpredictability means there's more risk, so it's important not to overpay and therefore try to build in a margin of safety.

I have previously covered what I refer to as hope, hype, potential stocks. These companies are all about what's to come. It's not about what they are currently doing – they are invariably losing money. It's the promise of what they can become. The power of these forces should never be underestimated, and they prevail to a different degree in most companies.

However, with big mature companies, it's more about what they are doing, which is generating lots of cash that they return to shareholders in the form of dividends or share buybacks.

You are never going to get rich owning these big mature companies unless you're already rich and the income you receive from them is meaningful. Most private investors are not rich. This is why hope, hype and potential stocks are so attractive to them. They believe these companies can make them rich.

This is not entirely inaccurate, but it's akin to swimming with sharks with the hope of grabbing one by their dorsal fin and riding it. You will be bitten. You will get some chunks taken out of you, especially if you do not have a robust risk/reward management strategy – and most private investors don't. This is why their investments can turn out to be financially fatal.

Big rewards in small places

The fact is, if you want to achieve a big reward, you have to look at smaller companies. As I previously mentioned, 60% of the best-performing companies started their run when their market capitalisation was below £100m. This does not mean you have to go for pre-revenue high-risk companies in order to achieve a decent reward. There are plenty of small listed companies that are decent businesses that are not high risk.

Size should not necessarily be associated with risk. This is like saying all small dogs constantly yap. Many don't. Mine doesn't – but the one over the road, who sits in the neighbour's front window, seems to bark all day.

Would a small growing company with a market capitalisation of £50m, with £20m of cash and no debt, be more of a risk than a company not growing valued at £1 billion market cap with £2bn of debt?

Of course, this is about the health of a company, which I mentioned earlier – but healthy, good improving small businesses should not necessarily possess outsized risk, just because they are small. The lack of a big risk also doesn't mean there's a lack of outsized reward.

It's a lot easier for a company below £100m market capitalisation to double in value than it is for one valued above £1bn. *Why?*

If a small company with a market capitalisation of £20m grows its topline for 20% over four years, its revenue would double. Let's say these revenues start at £10m; by year four they would be £20m. This is not market sector groundbreaking revenue generation. There are plenty of companies generating £20m in revenues, and the share of the market they inhabit is probably still quite small. So there's still plenty of market share to grab. This is very doable for a new-ish company, especially if its product or service is disrupting a sector. As the numbers get bigger, it becomes harder to replicate this type of growth.

Let's look at a bigger company with a market capitalisation of £1bn. If it starts with revenues of £500m, it would have to increase its revenues by £100m in the first year to achieve 20% growth. This compares to the smaller company, which only needs to increase its by £2m. A small gain in market share for a microcap can be very significant to its revenue. Whereas it would not be significant for a large company.

Big returns on big companies?

I am not saying you can't achieve outsized returns investing in big companies. You can – but it either takes many years, or you have to invest in a successful recovery play.

A good example of a big company recovery play is that of Rolls-Royce. On 12 October 2022 the share price hit a relative low of 65p. The share price had underperformed since 2018, compounded by Covid restrictions hitting profits. A new CEO was appointed in 2023 who undertook a major reorganisation. As I write this on 23 February 2024, the share price is 353p. That's a 440% rise.

So if you want to achieve big returns among bigger companies, recovery plays are the way forward – but they are not easy. Business turnarounds always take longer than expected and they come with many false dawns, which results in a very volatile share price. From October 2020, Rolls-Royce's share price hit a low of 39p, rallied to 143p by September 2021 and then fell to 65p by October 2022.

As I mentioned, the power of potential exists in most companies no matter what size they are. Rolls-Royce's volatility was largely down to the hope of recovery happening, buyers piling in and then selling when the company released an update suggesting that trading or the outlook has not picked up as expected.

When a business is not a business

A distinction has to be made between hope, hype and potential stocks and small businesses. Pre-revenue hope, hype and potential stocks are, in my opinion, not businesses. To be a business *you have to be doing business.* By this I mean selling a product or a service in return for revenue.

Pre-revenue hope, hype and potential stocks are not commercial. They have an idea or ideas they hope will become commercial. Don't get me wrong, this hope is powerful as it resides in the minds of the investors who are often prone to flights of fancy. And such exuberance is amplified a hundredfold across WhatsApp, Telegram or bulletin board groups; the excitement can reach fever pitch.

The power of potential is what moves a company's share price. A company can release a decent set of results, which are backwards-looking, but if the outlook statement in their release is gloomy the share price will tank.

This is why it's important to read the outlook statement and broker forecasts. How do you know what your return could be, if you do not know what the future potential is?

Forecasting the future

Potential is the estimated reward you can reasonably expect for risking your capital.

The potential generally stems from forecasts. But beware: forecasts are just that. Like weather forecasts, they are an informed estimate. They also become less accurate the more of the future they attempt to predict. A weather forecast for tomorrow has a high probability of being accurate. The further out the forecast tries to predict, the less reliable it becomes. This is the flaw in forecasts; they are never going to be completely accurate. But if they are based on reasonable assumptions then they can be a useful guide.

Forecasts also tend to be more accurate for bigger, mature businesses. These businesses are more predictable. Their models are proven and their revenue streams are diverse. In short, a lot less can go wrong (but things still can).

Brokers are generally paid by companies to write investment research. Of course, they have to be realistic – otherwise they would hold no credibility. But they also have to try to prove there's some decent investment potential. I have learned a lot about different sectors and the potential value of companies by reading broker notes. I would highly recommend any private investor attempt to get their hands on a note, especially one written about a company they have invested in. Valuing a company and its potential is a skill. It takes practice and reading broker notes is one of the best ways to learn. Due to me reading lots of these notes, over time, I have learned to create my own forecasts. Invariably my forecasts tend to rhyme with those of the brokers. However, on the occasions they don't sync and the broker's target price is way above my forecast, I become sceptical.

It's good to be sceptical. If you take a conservative view on forecasts and the potential is still very decent, then you know you are researching a company worth your time.

Forecasts are generally based on a multiple of certain metrics. The metrics used are dependent on what stage the company is at in its development.

The least accurate forecasts are those for pre-revenue companies because a lot of assumptions are baked in. Firstly, the assumption that the business will not only make it to the commercialisation stage – but that the sales suggested will materialise.

Beware of assuming this will happen. As I mentioned previously, I have invested in quite a few hope, hype, potential stocks that had (seemingly) promising products or technology but failed to get off the ground commercially. Some of them have gone completely bust, others are still trying to sell their wares. The resultant delay in getting to the market has meant extra fundraising rounds at bigger discounts for less money, while the share price tanks.

Never waste research

Potential is directly related to the current valuation. You can research a company and the potential may be partially priced in – but, if you like the business, it's always worth adding this company to your watchlist and applying chart alerts (more on this later). Share prices can be very volatile and a company at fair value today could become undervalued in a month's time. The trick is not to waste your research. If you have previously owned a company but got in at the wrong price and exited (or even if you got out at a profit) *keep an eye on it*. The stock market provides opportunities every day.

In summary, it will pay you to go for a lower, more achievable reward rather than a higher, less achievable one.

Part Three:
When

23.
When – Momentum

> "Under the tenets of behavioural finance, markets are not always efficient. It is human behaviour that moves markets and not the universal information shared by market participants"
> **—Gary Antonacci**

You can buy a good company at a bad price and lose money, and a bad company at a good price and make money. Your goal is to buy a good company at a good price and make lots of money.

This is how I approach investing, but it's a nod to Warren Buffett's quote:

> "It's far better to buy a wonderful company at a fair price than a fair company at a wonderful price."

My statement refers to both value and price, which are interlinked. If a share price goes up, so does the value of the company (I refer to value here as in the market capitalisation of the company) and so the potential goes down, unless the company's profit grows at the same rate or exceeds as the rise in the share price, in which case its valuation has not changed or it has become cheaper.

However, my version also refers to price – as in, the price on the chart. Before I get into charts, though, I would like to explore the best time to invest into a company from a fundamental risk/reward perspective.

As I mentioned previously, you are better off investing in a company releasing good news, even though the company's share price has rallied, than a company issuing a profit warning after the share price tanks.

So, firstly, stick with businesses that are improving, and by this I mean financially, not what the company's CEO is saying or its shareholders on social media or bulletin boards are claiming. Secondly, always be aware whether any news is due to be released on a company you intend to invest in (or top up on).

This applies to whether a company is a performer or a potential recovery play (especially recovery plays). Big news events can move the share price significantly and you do not know what the details of the news release is going to be. On my website I publish the date of each company's next set of financial results. This is an important piece of information to know.

Let's take an example. If you are convinced a performer is about to release another set of excellent financial results, check the chart. If the share price has rallied quite strongly, the market may have already priced in the good news.

Remember, lots of companies release trading updates a month or so before their full set of results. So a lot of the good news is known about. What isn't known about? Bad news – because trading updates tend to be the highlights. If there's anything in the full set of results that is a nasty surprise, the share price will drop.

Even if the full set of results does not provide more positive news than the trading update, the share price could fall. I have seen it happen so often. As the saying goes, "it's better to travel than arrive". There will also be investors who use big events like final or interim results as a liquidity event to exit. Hence the share price drops and doesn't reflect the positive news.

Even if the share price rises and you didn't invest before the news, it confirms the business is a good one and that it continues to perform. It removes the risk of further downside. In this case it's better to take a small holding after the rise and consider averaging up if the share price continues to perform.

Let's say you do the opposite and you take a big stake before the news. Only three things can happen:

1. share price rises

2. share price goes nowhere

3. share price drops.

If the share price rises, well done. However, as I mentioned before, most full-year or interim results are already priced in. The type of news that makes a share price move is *unexpected* news, either positive or negative. Like a positive trading update or a new contract.

Let's look at the other two options. The share price goes nowhere after the news – well, was it worth taking the risk?

Thirdly, the share price drops. You are sitting on a loss. When investing, if you do not get your entry correct, your exit is also unlikely to be correct. Now you're sitting on a loss, what do you do? Hope the share price goes up? Again, hope isn't an investing strategy.

Now picture where you would've been if you'd not bought and just waited for the news to be released. The stock would've dropped – and you have more information on the company.

This means the valuation of the company has dropped, but if the drop is just because the news is already being priced in or some are using it as a liquidity event to exit, the potential has also just gone up.

The more information you can get about a company before you invest, the better, as it derisks the investment. One of my biggest flaws as an investor is my lack of patience. I always tend to jump into stocks too early and go too big. This is fear of missing out, and focusing on the reward rather than the risk.

These mistakes are emotional investing and lack of risk management. If you are investing in a great business, it will be great for years. Not for days or weeks. Patience is discipline, the quality that separates exceptional investors from average ones.

I will give you a good example of this, where I tried to predict the momentum and got it wrong.

Example

A company I am currently invested in is called **Ramsdens (RFX)**. It's a diversified financial services provider and retailer, specialising in pawn broking, selling gold, foreign exchange and jewellery sales.

It's been a performer. From 1 January 2021 to June 2023, its share price rose by just over 100%. I invested on 3 January 2024 at 2.17p. On 15 January it released its annual results for the year ended 30 September 2023, which saw it achieving 27% topline growth to £83.8m and record pre-tax profit of £10.1m. It also had net cash of £13m and paid a 5% dividend. So it was on an EV/EBITDA of 5 and a P/E of 8. Therefore it possessed both growth and value.

The share price has dropped by 25% since it released these results.

Ramsdens – far from a pawn star

The chart here shows when it published its results and where I bought shares.

The smooth line you can see, which I cover later, is the 200-day moving average. You can see the share price was above this moving average for the entirety of 2023 up until August, where I have added an A on the chart.

Then it dipped below it, tried to rally, failed to make a new high – so this is a lower high and has been below the 200-day moving average since.

I thought it would break the 200-day moving average on its great results and bought in expectation on the morning of their release. It didn't. Never predict a future trend – wait for confirmation. You are better off being late to a great party than early to a rubbish one.

Charts

Many traditional investors disregard charts as some kind of voodoo dark art. I find this utterly perplexing. At its heart, the chart reflects money inflow and outflow in a company's stock. The share price is the truest representation of this.

This is what the stock market is all about: it's a marketplace where buyers and sellers meet. Share price movement is embedded in the most basic principles of economics – supply and demand.

I don't want to bore you with supply and demand charts but if there's lots of demand for a company's stock, and there's a lack of supply, i.e. lack of sellers, then the share price will rise.

This rise might encourage some sellers to accept the higher price and increase a bit of supply, but if demand still outweighs the supply the price will continue to rise.

If strong demand continues, there's net demand. If you are just looking at figures on a screen it is quite hard to identify this trend in buying or selling. This is where charts help.

The momentum that creates a trend can be more easily observed by using charts. There's no dark art to it, it is basic supply and demand economics. If you are a serious investor and you have done your fundamental research, why wouldn't you want to know if the actual stock of the company is in net demand (more buyers than sellers) or net supply (more sellers than buyers)?

It's not acceptable to say charts don't work. It's impossible for them *not* to work. They are more accurate and up to date than a company's financial statements. Financial results are three to six months out of date. Charts are a real-time reflection of the marketplace.

If you are a serious investor then your ultimate goal is to achieve a positive return on your capital. You do this by researching companies you think will provide you with this reward. Your capital is valuable, so allocation of it should not be done lightly. However, if you are not aware that a company's share price is in a downtrend due to persistent net supply, then your allocation of capital is inefficient. An efficient investment should give you a relatively quick return on your capital. This won't happen if the momentum of a company's share price is downward.

Which of these would you prefer? To see your investment reduce in value, even though the fundamentals seem to be improving? Or to wait until the downtrend has ended and a new uptrend starts, then allocate your capital?

Why would a company's share price be in a downtrend if its fundamentals are improving?

There are many reasons. Shareholders take positions in a company at all different price levels and across different time frames. There's no knowing what their personal goals or agendas are.

- You may have a big distressed seller, like a fund, who has to get out of all positions.
- The sentiment towards a certain sector may be negative, due to other companies releasing profit warnings. This could affect the company you are invested in if it's within that sector.
- The fundamentals may be improving but, if it's a turnaround recovery play, there could be longer-term holders underwater who just want out due to the long-term downtrend they've experienced. They may lack patience because they may have heard positive soundings from the company before but the recovery didn't come to fruition.

The thing is, it's not important to know the reasons why a share price is in a downtrend, it's just important to know if it is. If it is, but if all your other research on the company seems sound, **wait until the downtrend ends**. This way you will not see your capital erode. Even if it is a paper loss, it hurts emotionally.

A company that seems to be of good value can become one of excellent value, if its share price is in a downtrend – the potential becomes greater.

You have to make sure you are on the correct side of momentum because a rising share price tends to attract a growing number of buyers and a falling share price tends to attract a growing number of sellers. So momentum can build in either direction.

The chart is a graphical representation of net supply or net demand. There are only three basic states a share price can exist in:

1. downtrend

2. range

3. uptrend.

Consistent net demand creates an uptrend. Consistent net supply creates a downtrend. And if supply and demand are roughly equal, the share price will stay range bound, oscillating between an upper price and a lower price for an extended period of time.

So when you look at a chart, try to work out whether the share price is in an uptrend, downtrend or in a range. **All you need to do is avoid a downtrend.** If you are looking for capital appreciation (share price rising), rather than income (dividends) then you also need to avoid a range. If you are being paid a dividend to hold the stock, being in a range is not too bad. However, if you are only holding the stock with the expectation that the share price will rise, that is inefficient allocation of capital.

There's also the added worry that the share price could break the lower end of the range and start a new downtrend, which will attract more sellers and accelerate the fall.

Ranges tend to happen after an extended move in the share price, whether it be up or down. So if a company's stock has risen significantly over the last 12 months, then a period of consolidation needs to occur.

This could happen because existing investors who have done well want to take a profit because they may believe the potential is now fully priced in. However, you have new investors who believe there's more upside. So there's roughly an equal number of buyers and sellers.

The share price could break the top end of the range for a few reasons. It could be that sellers become exhausted but buyers don't, or the company could release some positive news, creating net demand for the shares.

The issue with buying into a range after a long downtrend is that you need a positive catalyst for the share price to break the range and enter a new uptrend. The share price could be in a range as sellers have become exhausted and there's little demand. If the company doesn't release any positive news, even recent buyers could exit and push the price into a new downtrend.

So it's safer to wait for the share price to break the upper range limit, to confirm a new uptrend has started, rather than just trying to predict it will.

When there's consistent net demand for a company's stock the share price will form a series of higher lows and higher highs.

This means previous highs (HH), which can sometimes be **resistance**, are broken.

Let's look at the key chart patterns you need to know and how to spot all this at a glance.

Uptrend

An **uptrend** signifies investors are constantly buying at higher prices. Even when some supply comes into the market and the share price dips, this supply is being bought up. Then the lack of supply, together with constant demand, pushes the share price to a new high.

The momentum builds as buying pushes the price up, which attracts more buyers, which moves the price even higher.

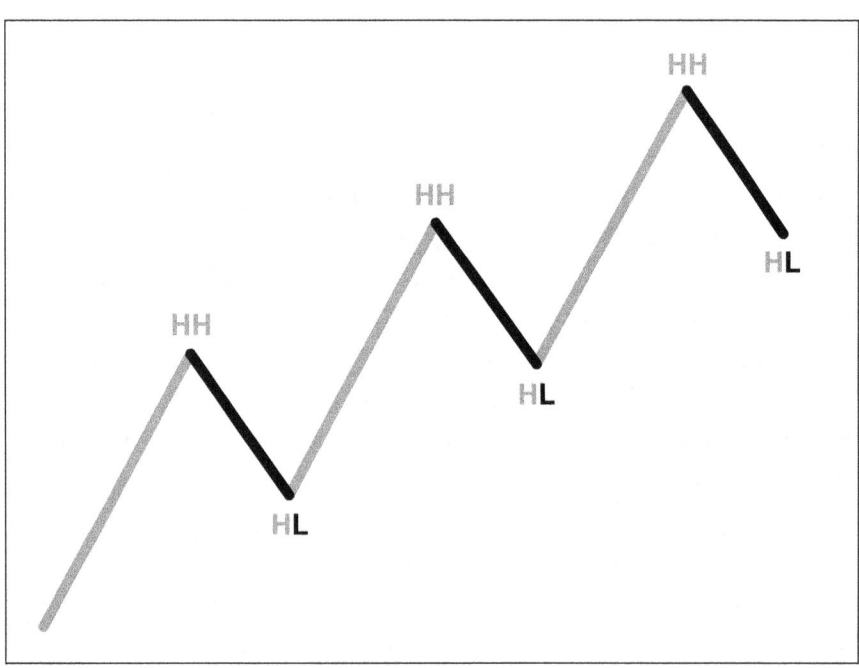

The friend of the uptrend

Downtrend

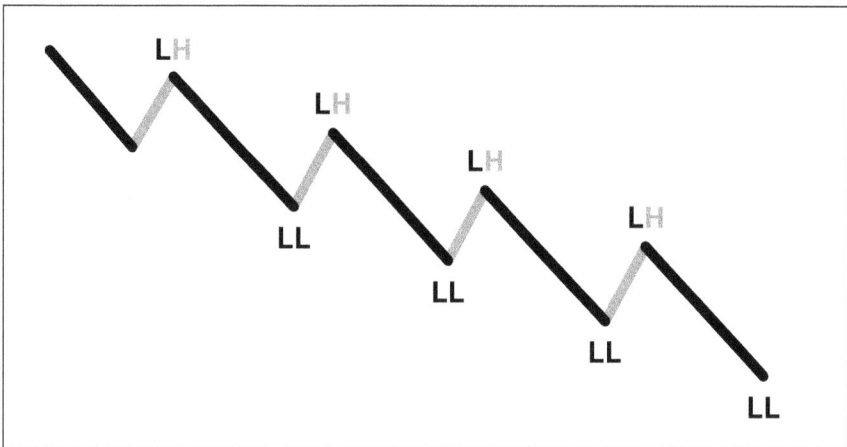

Feeling downtrend

The opposite of this is a **downtrend**. This shows that investors are constantly selling at lower prices. Even when some demand comes into the market and the share price rises, it's sold into and supply overwhelms demand. This lack of demand together with constant supply pushes the share price to a new low.

This means previous lows, which were **support**, are broken.

The momentum builds in a downward direction, as selling pushes the share price down, which encourages more sellers, pushing the price further down.

Range

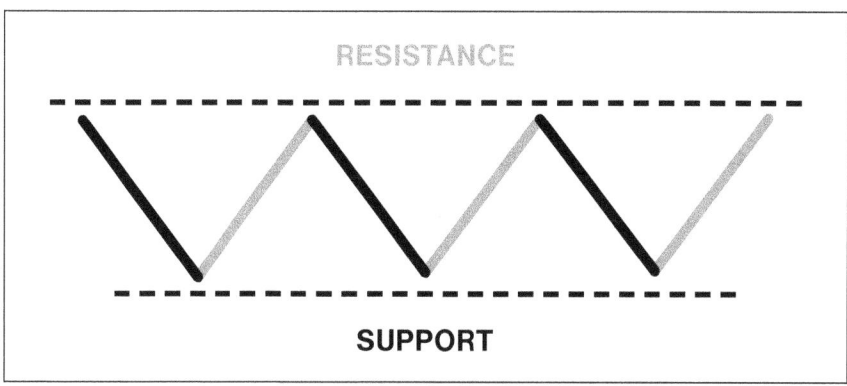

Hone in on the range

A **range** usually happens after an extended move by the share price in either direction. If it happens after a downtrend, sellers may either be slowing or buying has picked up and is equally matching them. If the range happens after a rally, it signifies buyers may either be slowing or selling has picked up and is equally matching them.

In short, it's a period of indecisiveness. The bulls and bears are having a tussle and who wins may depend on what news is released by the company. Personally, I try to avoid investing into shares when they are in a range for two reasons:

1. Ranges can last for a long time and investing in one is an inefficient allocation of capital. It's not so bad if the company pays a dividend because then you are being paid to hold the shares, but I predominantly invest for capital appreciation (share price ascension) not income.

2. There's no knowing in which direction the share price will break out of the range. You hope it will go through resistance into a new uptrend, but it could be the opposite. So you are better waiting for the company to break the resistance before investing.

How to assess momentum

Unless you are an experienced chartist, it can be difficult to pick out higher highs, higher lows, lower highs and lower lows. The trend is hard to spot as daily share price movements can be quite erratic. An easier way to observe whether a trend is occurring, and in which direction, is to use a chart indicator like a **moving average**.

A moving average is a smooth line that is calculated by plotting the average price over a certain number of days.

One of the most popular moving averages, often referred to as the *bull/bear line*, is the **200-day moving average**. It is calculated by plotting the average price over the last 200 days.

If the share price is above the 200-day moving average, it shows that investors are paying a price that is above the average share price over the last 200 days. This is bullish and is a good example of a company whose share price is gaining momentum. So whenever you look at a chart, your first check should be: is the share price above the 200-day moving average?

23. When – Momentum

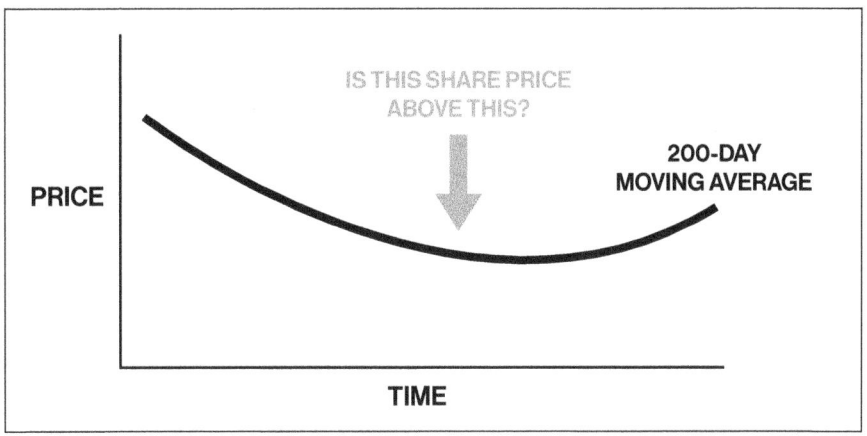

Red rag to a bull

Be careful, though, as it's not unknown, especially in smaller companies after a long oversold period, for the share price to violently spike up through the 200-day moving average, get sold into – and resume a downtrend.

What you want to see is the share price consistently forming a series of higher lows and higher highs above the 200-day moving average, and then the 200-day moving average also making a move upwards.

Below you can see a chart of **Next Plc (NXT)** after the Global Financial Crisis.

Next in crisis

The share price is represented by vertical lines called candles. Each candle represents the share price on a single day. If the candle is green the share price rose that day, if it's red, it fell (you may be reading this in black and white – don't worry as it's not important right now). As you can see, the share price is quite erratic so it's difficult to make out a pattern or trend.

The next chart is the same chart but I've added the 200-day moving average and annotated it with letters. Firstly, you can see the share price on the left of the chart at A, B, C, D and E is below the 200-day moving average.

At **A** the share price bounces, making this the first lower low. At **B** the share price peaks and instantly moves lower, due to net supply making **B** a lower high. **C** becomes the next lower low, **D** the next lower high and **E** the next lower low.

There's net supply and investors are constantly selling at lower price levels. Any demand gets drowned by more supply.

Remember, a falling stock price attracts sellers.

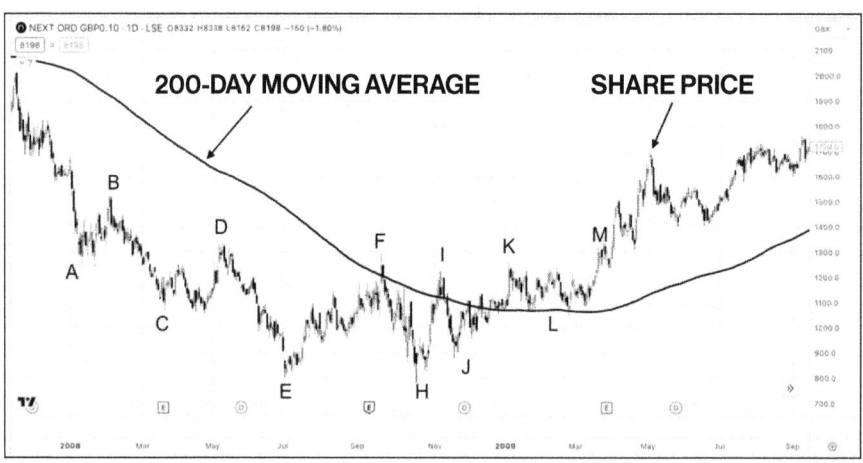

Next steps

At **F** the share price has rallied strongly and breaks the 200-day moving average. This is called a v-shaped recovery, which is often unsustainable. A more sustainable rise often needs to see the share price retest a previous low, maybe even present a higher low.

A to F, the 200-day moving average is also still sloping downwards. This is where the buyers and sellers are nearly equally matched, which means the share price can be a bit volatile. This often happens near a market bottom, as long-suffering investors underwater are using any bounce to exit.

At **H** the share price hits a low but it is not lower than the previous low. As I mentioned earlier, a higher low is a good sign a bottom may be in. It's a sign sellers are slowing or that buyers are increasing, meaning supply and demand are close to equilibrium

At **I** the share price breaks the 200-day moving average again but it only forms a lower high than F and the 200-day moving average is still slightly sloping downwards. However, on the sell off at **J** the price forms a higher low than the low at H, maybe suggesting supply is dropping off.

At **K** the share price has broken the 200-day moving average and the price manages to peak slightly above the previous high at I, which is a higher high, a bullish sign.

The lows at **L** do not revisit previous lows at J and H. J and L are higher lows. This suggests sellers are either dropping or the buyers are outnumbering them. The 200-day moving average is becoming flat.

At **M** you can see the share price makes a new high, above the previous peaks of F, I and K. This means there's net demand, the 200-day moving average starts sloping upwards and there's a series of higher lows and higher highs. This is the start of a new uptrend.

A rising share price attracts buyers.

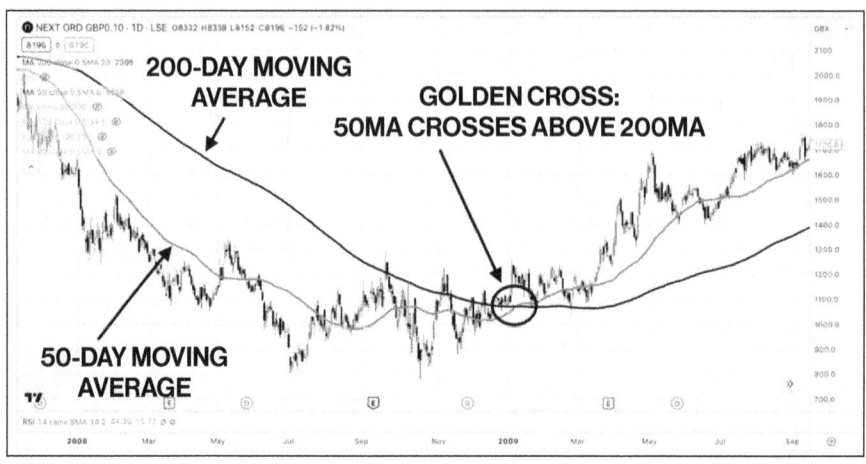

Next golden cross

Another moving average I add to the chart is the **50-day moving average**. The share price is averaged over 50 days so it is more reactive to the share price over a shorter time frame. However, when used in conjunction with the 200-day moving average it can prove to be a very useful indicator. As you can see above, when the 50-day moving average crosses up over the 200-day moving average, you can confidently say the downtrend has ended and the uptrend is about to begin.

This is a no-brainer study but work by US finance professor Seung-Chan Park in 2005 found that it was possible to predict the medium-term outperformance of a stock based on the ratio between its 50-day and 200-day MA.

His research showed stocks where the 50-day MA is higher than the 200-day MA tend to perform better than stocks whose 50-day MA is lower than the 200-day MA.

I will put it another way. The share price of **every stock** that becomes a winner has to rise above the 50-day moving average, the 200-day moving average and form a golden cross. **Every stock.**

Conversely, no stock becomes a winner if its share price is below the 200-day moving average. So seriously consider before taking a position in a company if this is the case. The only reason you should do this is if there's good momentum and the share price has broken the 50-day moving average and it is making a series of higher highs and higher lows.

23. When – Momentum

Here are some examples:

XP level up

This is the chart of **XP Factory (XPF)**. At **A**, where I started buying, you can see the share price breaking to new highs above the moving averages and the 50-day moving average crossing up over the 200-day moving average, forming the golden cross. From there, look how far above the 200-day moving average the price is. It also hardly touches the 50-day moving average. This is a powerful uptrend.

Then just before **B**, the share price dips and spikes through the 50-day moving average. You can put alerts on this happening. This would have provided you with the first warning sign. From there I should have inserted stop-losses locking in more of my profit. This way, if the share price had continued to rise, I would still be holding but would've exited if it went lower.

At B the share price is below the 50-day moving average. This is your second warning: the uptrend may be breaking down. Just after this the share price enters a bit of a range, trying and failing to make a new high. Meanwhile it also breaks down below the 200-day moving average (**C**). Previous to this, the share price hadn't touched the 200-day moving average since November 2020.

The bottom of the range was broken in December 2021, entering a new downtrend. I sold at around 15p, made 100%, but could've locked in another 100% if I'd just sold on the death cross (this is the opposite of the golden cross, where the 50-day moving average crosses down over the 200-day moving average). I became fixated on the narrative, not the numbers.

I got my entry right but my exit wrong.

Good Energy, great result

I bought **Good Energy (GOOD)** on 28 March 2023 at around 200p on the day it released its final results for the 12 months ended 31 December 2022. Revenue increased 70.3% to £248.7m, with profit before tax of £8.5m and cash in the bank of £24.5m. Its market capitalisation was £33.7m, net assets were £50.6m or £3 a share. Growth and value were present – and yet the share price failed to perform.

After an initial rally, it petered out. At B the price went below the 50-day moving average, while a golden cross was happening. If the share price is below the 50-day moving average when a golden cross happens, it negates the formation. This is because the price has to be *above* the 50-day moving average for that average to keep moving upwards.

At C, the death cross happened and by October I was 24% down. There was no significant news that moved the price up but at D it experienced six consecutive up days where it broke the 50-day and the 200-day. It also broke previous highs. This is classic net demand after

23. When – Momentum

sellers' exhaustion over an extended period of time. This means any demand would move the stock as there were very few sellers.

This was a good place to buy. You could also have put a 20% stop-loss in, in case it was a fake break. That stop would have only kicked in if the share price hit a new low.

Just after the golden cross happened between D and E it dipped but at E made another new high. This is bullish. Then it motored. Sometimes you get an early warning when a stock is about to drop. You see a sell off where the dip gets bought up but if the share price doesn't make a new high beware, as happened at G. Some of my stop-losses kicked in here. H was a lower high and was where it broke support. My stop-losses kicked in and I made a 60% profit.

I got my entry wrong but my exit was right.

Argentex it and entry

This is a chart of **Argentex (AGFX)**, a provider of currency management and payment solutions to international institutions and corporations.

I invested as it broke a new high, just before **A**. At **A** it released a trading update stating, "Argentex expects to report six month revenues of £27.4m, a 75% increase compared to the same period last year with costs remaining in line with management expectations. There has been continued strong client demand with the number of corporate clients trading growing to 1,393 (H1 2022: 1,241)."

The price gapped up and rose strongly. This is also where the golden cross occurred. There was some volatility on the way up, but the price didn't break the 50-day until **B**. First warning. At **C** the share price failed to make a new high. At **D** the price broke the 50-day again. Second warning: the trend is breaking down. At **E** the price tries and fails to close above the 50-day.

Even though **F** is a strong rally, it's a lower high than those of **C**. At F the company released a trading update: "trade in-line with the management expectations". This may not seem bad but they were exceeding expectations a few months back. This sent the price below the 200-day moving average and the death cross occurred.

I sold on 14 April at 120p for around 47% profit.

I got my entry and exit right.

Using charts for stop-losses

A few investors have mentioned to me that stop-losses do not work very well on microcap companies because they can be quite volatile.

It's true, small companies' share prices usually move a lot quicker than bigger companies' in both directions. Placing a stop-loss on any-sized company is a bit of an art. If you buy a company in a downtrend then your stop-loss may not be effective: it could get taken out within a few trading sessions.

When placing a stop-loss you have to have a high level of confidence that the share price will not breach it. So rather than just randomly placing a stop-loss 20% below where you buy a company, a little knowledge of charts is needed to work out whether this stop-loss will be effective.

One of the most effective positions for a stop-loss is below a defined level of support. Support is an area where the share price has bounced off and not gone below, ideally more than once.

Support can occur in a downtrend or during a pull back and consolidation in a share price after a rise. Share prices fall because there's net supply, i.e. there are more sellers than buyers. As the share price drops, so does the valuation of the company. At some point investors will regard the company's valuation as attractive enough to buy the shares. This, in conjunction with sellers slowing or becoming exhausted, means supply and demand cancel each other out. This is where support occurs.

The next step will hopefully be net demand, i.e. more buyers than sellers, which will move the share price up. Be careful, though, as a quick rise in the price off the support can also encourage sellers again, creating net supply and causing the share price to fall.

If this fall retraces back to the previous level of support and net demand occurs again, then this reveals a definite level of support and a level of resistance (where sellers appeared again after the rise).

Ideally, to create an uptrend, you would like the next rise in the share price to break through the level where sellers appeared after it bounced off support.

However, now you know there's a level of support you can buy – and, as long as your stop-loss is below this area, you can be relatively confident the share price will not drop to your stop-loss.

Here's an example:

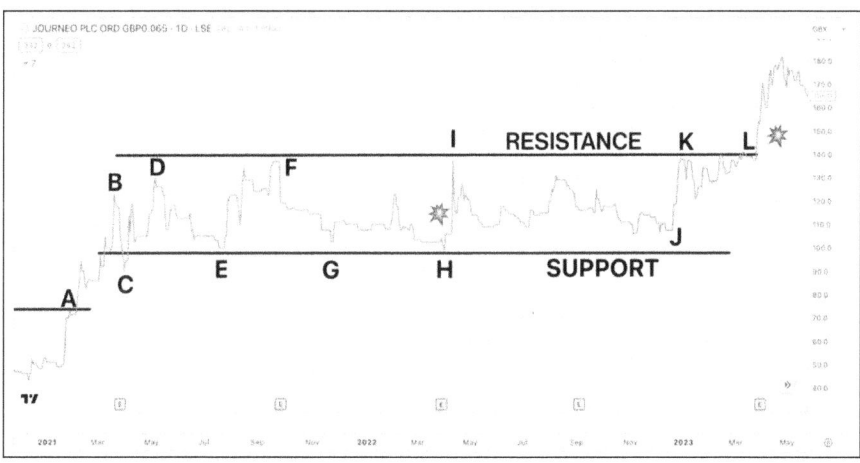

I want to break free

Early February 2021 the share price of a company called **Journeo (JNEO)** broke above previous resistance at 73p (**A**) and rose to 122p by March of that year (**B**). The share price then dropped to 90p by the end of March (**C**), due to profit takers, meaning there was net supply.

At this level buyers appeared and the share price rallied to 130p by May (**D**). From May 2021 to March 2022 the share price tested the 100p support area several times (**E, G, H** and **J**). It also tested resistance to the upper range several times (**F, I** and **K**). It never closed above 140p for 12 months. Then at the end of March 2022 the share price closed above this resistance. Finally, demand for the shares overcame supply and it broke above resistance.

From March 2023 to January 2024 the share price rose from 140p to 293p, a 110% rise. The best two places to buy this stock was either after a bounce off support, after **H**, or the break above resistance after **L**.

Stop, order time

Just after **H**, if you'd bought at 115p, then you could place your stop-loss 20% below at 92p, which is below previous support. You could safely assume, if it broke this level, a downtrend was likely to happen.

If you'd bought just after the break of resistance at 140p, then you could place your stop-loss at 112p. As it broke resistance at 140p, this now becomes the new support. Placing a stop-loss 20% below 140p would mean an exit should the share price drop to 112p.

So this is the **when** part of investing. If you know **how** to manage your portfolio and you know **what** to look for, this is **when** to invest.

Uptrend observation

- **Early indicator:** Is the share price above the 50-day moving average and making new highs?
- **Mid-term indicator:** Is the share price above the 200-day moving average and making new highs?
- **Confirmation:** Has the 50-day moving average crossed up over the 200-day moving average and is the share price still above the 50-day?

If a golden cross happens, make sure the share price is still above the 50-day moving average because, if it moves below it, this will drag down that moving average and could mean a death cross is going to happen, i.e. the opposite of a golden cross.

Downtrend observation

- **Early indicator:** Has the share price dipped below the 50-day moving average, especially after making a high?
- **Mid-term indicator:** Has the share price failed to make a new high, making lower highs, and is it dipping below 200-day moving average?
- **Confirmation:** Has the 50-day moving average crossed down over the 200-day moving average?

Don't be tempted to pick bottoms

Trying to pick the absolute bottom in a downtrend is a pointless obsession. I say obsession because I have tried to do it, as have many others. I suppose trying to nail the absolute low on a share price before it goes on a rally gives you some kind of macho bragging rights that "I picked the bottom on that one" but trying to do this will make you poor before it makes you rich.

Remember the aim of the game is to get a consistent return on your capital using metrics that make sense. It is not to try to guess where the bottom of a share price is. It shouldn't be a guessing game without skill. This is the equivalent to spending all your money constantly playing the lottery and shouting in loud celebration when you win a tenner now and then.

Sometimes investors do it because they want to try to get the maximum return they can. But it's a false economy. No one can guess the bottom or the top. Trying to predict these extremes means your returns will not be consistent – or, if they are, will be consistently down.

Because of momentum, selling attracts more selling and a previous low can be surpassed again and again and again, leaving you seriously out of pocket.

Trying to guess where the bottom is, is irrelevant. Working out if a downtrend has ended is more important. One low can be superseded by another low but a series of higher lows and higher highs makes a trend – and, once this starts, it's hard to stop it due to the momentum. So it's more meaningful and will provide you with better consistent returns.

At the bottom the share price is very volatile.

The low in Next occurred on 2 July 2008 at 837p. The golden cross happened on 8 January 2009 at 1195p. There was a 28% difference in these two points. But from the low occurring to the golden cross playing out, the share price rallied to 1247p in January and dropped to an intraday low of 780p on 17 October 2008. This is because around the bottom it becomes very volatile. So if you were genius enough to guess the bottom or thought you did, would you have held on even after it made a new low on 17 October?

If you'd just waited for the golden cross at 1195p and waited until the death cross happened, you would have sold out at 1978p on 26 August 2010 and collected a dividend. This is a 74% return, without dividends. However, the golden cross happened again on 16 June 2011 at 2278p and the death cross didn't until 19 November 2014 6656p. That's a 192% gain.

The clever bit is to do the fundamental research on a company, leaving you with the informed opinion that it's good value and there are early signs the business is recovering and going back into growth mode. Then you turn to the chart and wait until the downtrend has ended. A sideways range happens, then an upward breakout occurs and you buy a higher low or higher high after this move.

That is the mark of a good investor, not only fundamentally but technically – and in allocating your capital efficiently.

24.
Workflow

> "The individual investor should act consistently as an investor and not as a speculator."
> —**Benjamin Graham**

Setting up a system

In order to find opportunities, it's important to become organised. Good businesses are efficient and organised. You are looking to invest and become a shareholder in good businesses, so you have to treat your trading like a good business. This means you need to set up a system that not only finds investment opportunities but more importantly helps you not forget about them.

It's not good enough to just make a mental note of a company you think has potential; I guarantee you will forget about it. I know this because I have done so on many occasions, and it has cost me.

To do this you need to create an efficient workflow that gives you a good chance to uncover these opportunities and then record them in a way that reminds you about them when certain criteria are met.

Many investment opportunities might not be ripe for the picking straight away. A company could be fundamentally sound but its chart could be in a downtrend. You need reminding when the trend may be changing. Or you may have your eye on a recovery play. You do not want to miss the trading update that shows operations are finally turning around.

First off, you have to uncover these potential investments. How do you do this?

Uncovering potential investments

News

You can read through hundreds of company news releases every day, hoping to find a good company – but this is likely to become very tiresome very quickly, and it will get to the stage where you might not even know if you've read news that is significant.

The trick is to be a little more focused. There are thousands of listed companies out there. Not all of them are going to help you achieve your goal. So consider what you're looking for.

I used the analogy of a diamond miner previously but this is exactly what it's like. I know what I am looking for. I am searching for small, growing businesses at a good valuation that could go on to become superstocks. This is never going to be an easy task. Finding something exceptional is rare.

But it's going to be almost impossible to garner all this information I need from a single news release.

This is my morning routine.

Pre-market open

At 7am from Monday to Friday, one hour before the stock market opens for trading, listed companies – if they have any significant news – release it via the regulatory news service (RNS). This is not to say companies can't release news at any other time of the day but 7am is where the bulk of the news is released.

At 7am I will go to a website that publishes the daily RNSs. There's plenty of these but I usually use voxmarkets.co.uk, investegate.co.uk or londonstockexchange.com. Or I use the MicroCap News section on my website (stockpickers.com), which only publishes news from companies below a £100m market capitalisation. It also shows the market capitalisation of the company, the last reported revenue and the share price movement (after the market opens).

Watchlists

On the above websites you can create watchlists, which I would highly recommend you do. I have lots of different watchlists (normally ordered by market capitalisation), but I suggest you set up at least two distinctive lists: **owned** and **ideas**.

Owned

Owned are the companies I hold shares in. At 7am every weekday morning my first priority is to check whether any of these companies have released any news. I will be notified (from Vox Markets) or emailed (from Investegate and London Stock Exchange) if news from companies I own have released news. Next I move on to ideas.

Ideas

Ideas are companies I have researched and consider to have decent investment potential. This means I have run them through the growth, value, health, efficiency, momentum and potential filters on my website but am waiting on them to fulfil one or more of these criteria for me to invest.

The reasons I haven't invested in an ideas company yet could be one of the following:

- They have risen quickly and I believe the price will undergo a pull back and therefore improve the valuation and potential.
- The fundamentals are sound but the share price is in a downtrend.
- The company is a previous stock market winner but has suffered what I believe to be temporary headwinds and I am therefore waiting for them to recover.

Search

After having checked any news from my owned and ideas watchlists, I proceed to look for significant news from other companies. If I find what I believe to be news of interest, I will do a quick bit of research to see if the company fits some of my filters. The types of news I am looking for are:

- full-year results
- interim results
- trading updates
- contract wins.

Research

The first metric I observe is **market capitalisation**. If the company is below £100m (or up to 10% above) I research further, specifically whether it passes my growth, value, health, efficiency, momentum and potential filters.

Here's a quick summary of what I look for in regards to these metrics:

- **Growth**: I look for double-digit revenue growth, ideally closer to 20% than 10%. I want to see profit growing at a similar rate too. I also look to see whether a company has more cash this year than last year, generated from operations (as opposed to equity issuance or debt).
- **Value:** A market capitalisation of less than two times its revenue (price to sales <2) and less than 20 times net revenue (P/E).
- **Health:** Ideally a company will have little debt, and net cash.
- **Efficiency:** I would like gross margins to exceed 40%, operating margins to exceed 10%, and net margins to exceed 5%.

These metrics would fit a company I have previously termed a performer. For a recovery play, the quality bar would not be as high. I would still be looking for an improvement across these same metrics but not to the same extent. I would look to historical figures to see if they had achieved these levels in regards to growth and efficiency.

If I am convinced a company does pass these filters, there's a chance I could invest that morning. However, these opportunities are very rare. There are only two situations where, after a company releases news at 7am, I would invest in the company at 8am.

1. I know the company, having previously researched it, and have been expecting this news or it's news that significantly improves the company's potential. Having previously researched the company is important, because I will already know a lot about the company's growth, its valuation, health, efficiency, potential and momentum. For example, if I've already researched a company, quite liked it and they release news detailing a significant contract win that could mean they are currently undervalued, I will invest.

2. The news is very good and the company, largely, fits my six metrics. This happened recently. A company released news entitled, 'Significant Contract Wins and Trading Update'.

The company was called **Beeks Financial Cloud (BKS)** and stated:

> "Beeks Financial Cloud Group plc is pleased to announce the signing of a multi-million-dollar, multi-year expansion contract for its Proximity Cloud offering, a new win with its Exchange Cloud Offering, and provide an update on a period of continued positive trading momentum in the six months to 31 December 2023.
>
> "Having won a number of competitive tenders in H1 FY24, the Company now expects trading in FY25 to be significantly ahead of previous Board expectations for FY25."

The company went on to outline an extension of an existing contract and a new contract with one of the largest exchange groups globally. Its trading update stated it would be achieving topline growth of 25% year on year with better margins, reaching free cash flow status, and that its cash level had increased from £4.4m to £5.5m.

This was not a one-off lucky contract. It said to me the business was improving on multiple fronts. The share price rose by 18% on the opening bell but I managed to get up to my 3% total portfolio value. Currently I am up over 20%.

Post-8am market open

If I do not find any news I believe to be particularly significant, I use the market's reaction as a filter.

Good news normally moves companies' share prices higher, while bad news has the opposite effect. This is the market's way of showing you what it thinks of the news. I do this by looking at the big risers of the day.

Some investors tend to think the best place to look for bargains is to search for the big fallers of the day, trying to find a quick opportunity by jumping into an oversold company. Whenever you look into the bargain bucket in the shop, it's the items people didn't want, hence why they have been reduced. Many of these items go unsold for weeks or months because, even at their new reduced price, they are probably not worth it.

I would like to reiterate what I discussed earlier. You are looking for businesses that are improving. Companies that release bad news tend not to be improving. Also a bad news release, like a good news release, usually does not exist on its own. If a company issues a profit warning, it's not one and done. It's symptomatic of a deeper issue within the company or the sector it is operating in. Conversely, when a company releases good news, it's a sign the business operations are headed in the right direction.

If a company releases bad news it usually means the company is going to generate less revenue/profit. The share price drops to try to reflect this. It's hard to evaluate if a company is a bargain on the day the price drops after a profit warning because this probably will not be the last one. If there are further profit warnings, the company will be worth less and the price needs to drop further to accommodate this. So it's nearly impossible to weigh up whether a company, undergoing a downgrade in earnings, is a bargain or overvalued. The best thing to do is to step back and await further information.

Normally a company will release a trading update announcing a profit warning. This trading update is a summary of its next set of results. So when its results come out, it's another release of bad news. Will the next trading update be more positive? Is it worth investing first, hoping it is, and taking the gamble? A lot of traders do but this is called *catching a falling knife*. Do you really want to take part in such a risky situation? Hope is not an investment strategy. Wait for confirmation with further news.

I liken a profit warning to an athlete who has suffered a serious physical injury. They will not get back to fitness straight away. It will take months of rehabilitation to get back to the stage where they can compete at the top level they were performing at previously. If they are of a certain age where injuries are an occupational hazard they may never get back to competing at that level. Some companies may never recover to their previous form. This is the risk you take jumping into a company issuing a profit warning.

I do look at the biggest fallers but never with the intention to immediately invest in them. More on this later – but back to the biggest risers of the day. I only observe the risers of the day to potentially add to my ideas watchlist and *not* to invest.

The biggest riser and the biggest fallers are both extremes. To generate consistent returns, try to avoid extremes. You need to search for consistency.

Investing in big risers, especially soon after the market opens, can end badly. When the market immediately opens, stock price movements are more exaggerated. This is because a company's shares can go from below average daily volume the previous day, to no volume prior to the market opening, to extreme volume on open. Market makers, who are the middle people between the buyers and sellers, are overwhelmed with demand for stock. This is economics 101. If there's limited supply but surging demand, the price will rise. So be very careful about taking a position in a company as soon as the market opens, especially if the share price moves up a lot higher straight away.

You will often find, around 60 minutes after the market opens, a bit of supply comes into the market, which results in the share price pulling back from its high. So if you are convinced in the investment potential of a company after it has just released news and can't get a position in the first half an hour, or it's risen aggressively, wait.

Only take a position within the first 30 minutes if you are 99% convinced the news the company has released means the company is very undervalued even after the share price has risen and you think it's likely to go higher, that day and the next. Like I said, you will normally be able to get a better price an hour after the market has opened.

Invariably I will not take a position in a company that appears among the biggest risers of the day. Share prices never go straight up. There's always a pull back. If there isn't a big enough pull back, there are always other opportunities.

This is where fear of missing out can become very powerful. You have to resist this feeling. It's where discipline needs to be exercised. Your ability to suppress this emotion will determine whether you will become a very good investor or an average to bad one.

In my experience, there are two ways to extinguish fear of missing out.

1. Buy a tiny amount of stock.
2. Add it to your ideas watchlist and put a chart alert on the price.

Investing in a company on the day it releases news is one of the best ways to attain a company at a bad price. On average, a company will release news less than once a month. The day on which it releases good news, the share price will rise strongly. Unless the news is absolutely transformational, you would be better off investing in a company on a no news day.

Market close

I usually check the risers and fallers again, just in case a company has released news throughout the day that I might have missed. I will also look at the MicroCap News section on my website for the same reason.

Chart alerts

I use a platform called TradingView for my charts and alerts. In fact, to say TradingView is just a chart platform greatly undersells the powerful functionality of its platform. It also shows company fundamentals, broker forecasts, screeners and a lot more. It's a very powerful platform worth taking the time to get to know (see the next chapter: Resources).

I pay for the package I use but there is a basic package that is free to access. The more you pay, the more functionality you get – but if you are new to charts the basic free package is fine.

I will replicate the watchlists on TradingView that I have on the other websites.

Biggest fallers

I only ever look at the biggest fallers with the hope of spotting a decent recovery play, that *might* happen many months down the road.

I say *might* because it isn't a guarantee. When a company issues a profits warning, it usually signifies that something is not working within the business. The alternative reason is macro headwinds within the sector or a global slowdown affecting the company's fundamentals. Whatever the reason, it is never just a one-day problem. It's more likely to be a one-year problem.

If I see a previously good company take a hit, then I will add a chart alert to it. The alert I use is as follows: **share price crossing the 50-day moving average**.

24. Workflow

This could just be a technical bounce and the share price could resume a downtrend soon after, but it alerts me to a movement that might be sustainable. This alert lets me know that the share price of the company might have hit a bottom or is in a bottoming process. The chance of this being the case is around 50/50. So it's not a high level of confidence, but it reminds me about the company and serves as a cue to quickly research the company again.

To create this alert, select: **control** and click on one of the share price candles. A dialogue box appears, select, "Add Alert on [COMPANY NAME]".

Click the **price** drop-down menu and select, "MA (50 close)".

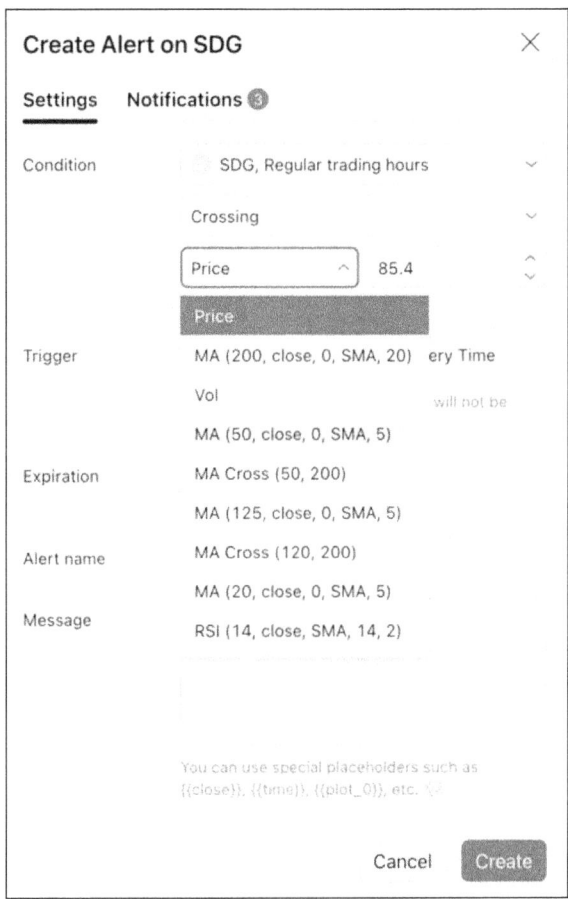

Creating an alert

Another alert I use: **share price crossing the 200-day moving average**. This alert is closer to confirmation that a share price is recovering from a downtrend and may be moving into an uptrend, but it could be just a technical bounce which reverts to a downtrend. If it is a technical bounce then it's normally v-shaped; this is usually not sustainable. A u-shaped recovery in the share price is a lot more sustainable, especially if the price crosses the 200-day moving average and makes some higher highs and higher lows.

To create this alert, select: **control** and click on one of the share price candles. A dialogue box appears, select, "Add Alert on [COMPANY NAME]".

Click the **price** drop-down menu and select, "MA (200 close)".

Whenever I receive an alert notification it reminds me to revisit that company and do another bit of research, just to check it does still possess decent upside potential.

Screeners

Screeners are another way to find potential investments. These are tools that allow investors to sort through thousands of individual stocks to find those that fit their own criteria or methodologies. As I mentioned previously, there are far too many companies on the stock market to research, so screeners help you whittle down the list. The key to using screeners is to know what you are looking for before you start playing around with them. Otherwise you will keep fiddling around with the filters for ages and forget what you were originally looking for.

So if you are looking for small growth companies at a reasonable valuation, start with a filter that only shows companies below a certain market capitalisation. Then set two more filters, one to look for companies that possess topline growth, say above 10%. Then set the other filter to display companies that have an EV/EBITDA below 10. You will have already weeded out hundreds of companies.

Weekends

If I have not checked my stops throughout the week I try to check them on the weekend. I use Google Sheets to manage my portfolio. I have become a huge fan of Google Sheets over the last few years. They

24. Workflow

are an excellent resource to help you select and manage your stocks (see the next chapter).

I do this primarily to manage the risk and reward. If you hold over ten stocks then you can often lose track of a share price, whether it's risen or fallen throughout the week. With Google Sheets these movements can all be highlighted automatically when a stock meets certain conditions.

		PROFIT / LOSS (%)	HOLDING (%)	FIRST BOUGHT	PRICE (p)	BUY PRICE	STOP 1	PROFIT / LOSS AT STOP (%)
1	Beeks Financial Cloud	39.95%	13.3	06/02/24	£2.64	£1.89	£2.08	10%
2	Billington Holdings	3.98%	1.2	09/07/24	£5.25	£5.05	£4.04	-20%
3	Cambridge Cognition	10.83%	1.9	11/07/24	£0.45	£0.41	£0.37	-10%
4	Celebrus Technologies	10.73%	1.3	09/07/24	£2.86	£2.58	£2.32	-10%
5	Eneraqua	-15.28%	1.2	07/06/24	£0.405	£0.478	£0.38	-20%
6	Facilities by ADF	-2.46%	2.0	23/01/24	£0.54	£0.55	£0.44	-20%
7	Good Energy	-9.39%	1.1	14/06/24	£2.45	£2.70	£2.30	-15%
8	Manolete Partners	0.16%	1.6	18/04/24	£1.45	£1.45	£1.16	-20%
9	Premier Miton	2.14%	1.7	01/07/24	£0.74	£0.72	£0.58	-20%
10	Ramsdens	11.17%	9.6	26/03/24	£2.33	£2.0914	£1.78	-15%
11	Synectics	11.58%	3.0	06/08/24	£2.01	£1.7978	£1.59	-12%
12	Time Finance	31.62%	7.0	28/11/23	£0.54	£0.41	£0.45	10%
13	ISHARES UK DIVI ETF	8.55%	9	24/05/23	£7.67	£7.07		
14	Vanguard Short-Term Money Market	-0.03%	11	16/07/24	£1.00	£1.00		
15	UK GOVT BOND 22/10/2061	1.86%	17	23/07/24	£0.31	£0.31		
16	USD Corporate 1-3 Year Bond	-2.96%	17	31/07/24	£37.35	£38.49		

Action between the sheets

25.
Resources

"It amazes me how people are often more willing to act based on little or no data than to use data that is a challenge to assemble."
—**Robert Shiller**

Resources

Google Sheets / Microsoft Excel

There's a huge amount of functionality within spreadsheets and they are what I base the MicroCap League on. You are able to pull into them all the information you need, including the following data: stock prices, volume, market cap, highs, lows, P/Es, earning per share, moving averages, etc.

If you learn to add formulas and conditional formatting, it can seriously enhance your portfolio management. For example, I can easily see by using conditional formatting and colours when a share price is up or down a certain amount, or when it is at a level I should consider averaging up or cutting if I haven't placed a stop in correctly. I would seriously urge you to learn to use spreadsheets if you don't know already. Google Sheets are free to use, all you need is a Google account.

Websites

TradingView

Charts, Alerts, Risers, Fallers, Financials, Forecasts, Date To Next Results, Screeners.

I probably use this website more than any other. It's very useful. Do not make the mistake that it's just about charts. Yes, it is the best chart platform out there, with thousands of different settings/indicators. It also has data on companies' fundamentals and excellent screeners.

Stockopedia

On a daily basis, Stockopedia features excellent coverage of small cap companies. I really like Paul Scott's coverage, especially his podcast. Paul is an investor who has done well over the years so he's worth listening to. Stockopedia also features excellent breakdowns on company fundamentals, company comparisons, forecasts and screeners.

Investegate

Investegate supply RNS news delivered by email or on its website. You can also add your own list. I have a list that pretty much follows all revenue-generating companies below £100m market capitalisation. You can also search for RNSs under certain categories, e.g. Results, Trading Updates.

Investing.com

Watchlists, Price Alerts, Volume Alerts, Notifications, Macro New Calendars.

SharePickers.com

Come on, I can't not mention my own site! I do a weekly live webinar for members, post updates on MyWatchlist, run the MicroCap League (where 100 microcaps below £100m market cap are ranked according to growth, value, health, efficiency, momentum and potential), and share MicroCap News.

Vox Markets

RNS delivered by notification, fund manager interviews, podcasts.

To become a better investor I believe you always have to want to learn. Not only about businesses but the macro environment and how it impacts businesses. It's important to immerse yourself in business news and investing. These days you can learn wherever you are. When I do my daily dog walk I listen to podcasts.

Podcasts

Wake Up to Money – BBC Radio 5 Live

Sky Business News Podcast with Ian King

Merryn Talks Money – Bloomberg

Small Caps Podcast with Paul Scott

The Fund Your Retirement Podcast

On the Money – Kyle Caldwell

The SharePickers Podcast – Justin Waite ;-)

Books

Stock Market Wizards by Jack D. Schwager

The Naked Trader by Robbie Burns

100 Baggers: Stocks that Return 100-to-1 and How to Find Them by Christopher W. Mayer

The Art of Execution: How the world's best investors get it wrong and still make millions by Lee Freeman-Shor

One Up On Wall Street: How To Use What You Already Know To Make Money In The Market by Peter Lynch

26.
The End is the Start

> "It ain't about how hard you hit. It's about how hard you can get hit and keep moving forward; how much you can take and keep moving forward. That's how winning is done!"
> **—Rocky Balboa**

Finally, you've probably guessed that I love good quotes. I believe they distil the truth and that's the reason they resonate. Every quote I've used in this book has come from an investor but this last quote comes from a boxer, or to be more accurate an actor/director who played a boxer – but it's so relevant when it comes to investing.

The reason this quote is so apt is because success in investing is less about picking winners than it is about avoiding big losers.

Recently Anthony Joshua fought Francis Ngannou, a former mixed martial arts fighter who held a record for the hardest-hitting punch. Ngannou has held this record since 2017. He registered a striking power of 129,161 units on a PowerKube (which measures the power of a punch by analysing its force, speed and accuracy). The last person that tried to overthrow the MMA star was the former World's Strongest Man winner Eddie Hall, but he failed.

UFC president Dana White emphasised just how powerful the MMA star is by comparing his punches to being struck by a "12-pound sledgehammer from full-force overhead".

Anthony Joshua dominated the bout, knocking down Ngannou with a straight right hand in the first round. Ngannou beat the count but was floored again in the second round. He rose to his feet, but Joshua finished the fight with another right hand that left Ngannou flat on the canvas for several minutes afterwards.

The point is, it doesn't matter how powerful your punch is, it's going to be useless if your defence is lacking. This is the same with investing. It does not matter how many winners you pick, if you hold more losers or your biggest holding is a loser, you will not make money.

So make sure your losers stay small. How do you know which stock will be a loser? You don't until they start losing. When you make a new investment you assume it will be a winner, otherwise you would not invest in it – but some will turn out to be losers. Do not decide you have a winner before it starts winning. Otherwise you are likely to go too big on this investment. Then if it turns out to be a loser, you will get in trouble.

This is the same with winners. You are never going to be 100% sure which company will be a winner, until they start winning. As I said earlier, it's the same as trying to guess the winning horse before a race starts. It's a lot easier to spot which horse is likely to win after the race is underway. *You can do this with investing.* That's why it's important to start small and let the winners and losers reveal themselves. If they turn out to be a loser, make sure you cut before it becomes too big. If it turns out to be a winner, increase your exposure.

In a wider context, there will never be a perfect time to invest. There will always be risks, there will always be wars and economic worries – but if you pick the right companies and position your portfolio appropriately, you can make money in all these environments.

I often believe that, where there's a negative, there's a positive. Losing my job and nearly losing my mortgage deposit was in retrospect one of the best things that happened to me. I had no other option than to get better at investing. If I had walked straight into another job I probably would never have focused so much of my time and effort on investing.

Likewise the recent bear market has been one of the longest and most brutal I can ever remember. The top of the market on AIM was on 6 September 2021 and as I write this on 23 April 2024, 959 days later, it is still in a bear market. From the high to the low the index fell by 49%.

There's been lots of talk that the Alternative Investment Market (AIM) and the wider UK stock market may never recover as many companies have delisted or moved their listings to the US.

I do not believe this. I think it's a natural function of the markets. At the top of the market, many new companies list on the stock market because everyone is optimistic, believing the market can only go higher, and therefore willing to invest. Whereas at the bottom of the market, the opposite is true; everyone is fearful, believing it will go lower, and very risk averse.

In short, people are always doing the very opposite of that old adage, "buy low, sell high".

It could be argued that companies delisting are not of good quality. The low interest rate environment created by the central banks for the last 12 years allowed businesses with weak business to survive. These businesses were largely subpar and un-investible. AIM needs quality not quantity.

I am highly confident the market will rally and recover, encouraging net inflows and laying the ground for new companies to list. Staying on the 'every negative has a positive' theme, I believe this is one of the best times to invest. There are lots of good businesses at great valuations potentially presenting an opportunity only seen once in a decade.

The path to freedom

You can make lots of money investing in the stock market.

If you look at the average person earning a regular wage, their take-home pay is all they will ever earn. This wage dictates what they can afford. Some people are prepared to accept this. For others, knowing you are limited in this way can be very frustrating. If this is you, the good news is, you can do something about it.

If you become a good stock picker you can turbo charge your take-home pay by many multiples. There's no ceiling to what you can earn. If you have read this far, I assume you want to find a way to do this.

There's only two realistic ways in life to create your own wealth: by owning a good business or by owning a share of a good business.

When you work for someone else, they are paying you what they think you are worth. It is determined by market economics. Any pay increases will also be dictated by this. Your employer is unlikely to suddenly say, "We believe you should be paid twice what we pay you now". If you are lucky your wage will increase by the rate of inflation.

If you want to achieve a better standard of living, if you want to buy the house you have always dreamed of owning, you will not do it by receiving a regular wage and just accepting that's your lot. You have to take that money and make it work for you. You've worked for that money, make it work for you. Yes, there's a risk – but reward does not exist without it. Anyone who has ever been successful has taken risks. As far as we are aware, we only have one life. There are plenty of people in this world who, for many different reasons, are not fortunate enough to be in a position to be able to invest money. You are lucky enough to be in that position. Do not waste your opportunity.

If you follow the rules in this book, you can turbo charge your pay at a smaller risk. This boost in your wealth can be done by investing it in the right companies listed on the stock market.

Finding the right companies means you have to learn the skills to become a good investor. It's not about following others' tips or ideas, it's about developing your own skills to be good enough to find your own investment ideas. Once you have these skills they will always be with you and no one can take them off you.

But in order to develop these skills you have to put in the effort, because these skills cannot be taught, they have to be learned. This learning takes effort but it is worth it. If you put the effort in, I know for a fact you can transform your life.

Why do I believe this?

Because I have transformed my life through investing and I am not a one off. I am an ordinary person, with no special qualification, who has a passion for investing. If you have the same passion, you too can create your own wealth independent of anyone else. As long as the stock market opens, you can make money.

26. The End is the Start

And just one last time, private investors lose money because of these two reasons:

1. They go too big on the wrong stocks and hold on to these losers too long.
2. They sell their winners too early.

Don't make these mistakes. Here's a quick summary of the principles outlined in my three-step strategy:

✓ What – Fundamental Analysis

Look to invest in improving businesses that are growing and of good value. By improving I mean the figures, not the management's vision or your perception.

✓ When – Technical Analysis

Never buy a company in a downtrend, regardless of the fundamentals. Momentum is a powerful force in both directions. A rising share price attracts buyers, a falling share price attracts sellers.

✓ How – Portfolio Management

This is the most important part about investing that is very rarely referred to. Firstly, a low-cost, well-diversified fund should be the backbone to your portfolio. You should invest a regular amount into this fund, preferably on a monthly basis.

When it comes to investing in individual companies, make any new investment small. Focus on the risk first, not the reward. That way if it goes wrong, you are prepared and your loss will be small. There will be plenty of time to average up on any extraordinary winners. By doing this your portfolio value will be leveraged towards your winners, not your losers.

Hopefully this book has provided you with some value and will be the start or the re-start of your investing career.

Contact Me

Ratings and reviews

If you genuinely liked this book, please give it a top rating and review on Amazon. You could receive a year's free membership to the SharePickers Investment Club!

If you would like to contact me, you can do so via email: justin@sharepickers.com

Or on social media:

- x.com/SharePickers
- www.youtube.com/channel/UCpBSO3c4D1H0D35eg40RwpQ
- www.linkedin.com/in/justinadamwaite

SharePickers

If you would like more help or information on investing in UK MicroCaps then visit my Investment Club.

www.sharepickers.com

Acknowledgements

When I completed this book, I casually asked if any members of my Investment Club would like to read it to check for spelling or grammatical errors. I was blown away by the level of detail Mark Varley and Geoffrey Lowe replied with. Thank you so much for not only reading the book so quickly but for sending me your fastidious notes. One part of me was thankful but another part of me thought, *Was this book even readable before your corrections?*

I also owe Pete (from the Weekend Podcast) thanks for doing the same too. Although he was a bit more laid back about it, sending me pictures of him sunbathing in Spain saying, "I could do with a good book to read now."

Printed in the USA
CPSIA information can be obtained
at www.ICGtesting.com
JSHW010739251024
72386JS00002B/2